m4.

rtha, Co
PY

Cork City Library
WITHDRAWN
FROM STOCK

244748

The Book of
Irish Golf

The Book of
Irish Golf

JOHN REDMOND

GILL & MACMILLAN

218606

Gill & Macmillan Ltd
Goldenbridge
Dublin 8
with associated companies throughout the world

© 1997 John Redmond
0 7171 2526 2
Print origination and design by Design Image, Dublin
Printed in Hong Kong

All rights reserved. No part of this publication may be
copied, reproduced or transmitted in any form or by any
means, without permission of the publishers.

A catalogue record is available for this book from the
British Library.

1 3 5 4 2

CONTENTS

FOREWORD

I make no apologies for the re-telling of my favourite story about Irish golf. It recalls a fine summer's day at the holiday resort of Lahinch, that famous village in County Clare, often referred to as the St Andrew's of Irish Golf. A couple of American visitors were enquiring about the chance of a game with some local members.

'Certainly,' assured the club secretary, 'Brud' Slattery. 'I'll play with you and I'll send one of the caddies up to the village to fetch the butcher.'

In due course, another renowned Lahinch character, Mick O'Loughlin, arrived and after he had nonchalantly wiped clean his blood-stained hands on his apron and teed-off, one of the bemused visitors turned to Slattery and whispered: 'Say, if the local butcher is so readily available to play golf, he sure can't make much money.'

To which 'Brud' replied: 'No, but he sure makes a lot of friends.'

To me, that story goes a long way to capturing the essence of Irish golf and it illustrates just why Ireland is revered the world over as a unique golfing location.

It is estimated that more than 300,000 people are actively involved with golf in Ireland, but this number can be multiplied greatly if golfing visitors are taken into account. And while tourism adds immeasurably to the national economy of the country, it has a particularly beneficial impact on golf.

What will the visitor find? First of all, an astonishing variety of courses, from classic links with long honourable histories, to leafy park-land courses, some of which are of a very recent origin. Many of these links and courses have been enthusiastically endorsed by the great commentators; or have been designed or modified by world renowned names.

The spirit of Old Tom Morris, H.S. Colt, James Braid and Alister Mackenzie fills the senses from times long past, their venerable contributions being further augmented by the august hand of Jack Nicklaus, Arnold Palmer and Robert Trent Jones in more modern times.

The visitor will also find a warm welcome at golf clubs throughout Ireland, where hospitality is a by-word, and where warm-hearted members are happy to share not only their facilities, but also their frequently colourful history.

In the past three decades, golf in Ireland has experienced extraordinary growth. Once considered a fairly élitist sport, the game that evolved well over a century ago from among the well-heeled classes of British aristocracy and with a distinct Scottish flavour, is now hugely popular as evidenced by the vast numbers wanting to play and in tandem with new courses developed or under construction.

It is witnessed also by the large and enthusiastic galleries at tournaments and the genuine popularity of golfing champions, be they amateur or professional. Where history shows that the formative years of Irish golf was blessed by the participation of such legends as Herd, Vardon, Taylor, Braid and Ball, it is further enhanced by the regular visits of today's giants of the game.

So, the reality of modern Irish golf is a complementary tapestry of many hues and hopefully *The Book of Irish Golf* accurately reflects that complexity and colour.

John Redmond

ACKNOWLEDGMENTS

The author acknowledges the assistance of: Frank Johnstone; Seamus Smith, General Secretary, GUI; Maureen Madill; Pat Ruddy; Simon Tormey; Bord Failte; Northern Ireland Tourist Board; Paddy O'Looney, SWING; Michael Burke; Ireland West; Alistair Smith; Michael Neary; William Gibson (*Early Irish Golf*), Dermot Gilleece (*Illustrated History, ILGU*); William A. Menton (*GUI Centenary Year Book*); John Hanna.

The publishers are grateful to the following for permission to reproduce photographs on these pages:

pages 34 (bottom), 36 (left), 71 (middle), 71 (bottom left), 72, 74 (bottom), 75 (bottom), 80, 81, 86 (right), 87 (bottom), 88, 119 (bottom), 147, 152 Allsport Photographic Ltd, © Allsport; page 38 (bottom) Allsport Historical Collection, © MSI; page 76 Associated Press Ltd; pages 25, 28, 134 (bottom), 148 Bord Failte; pages 9 (top), 12 (top), 14 (bottom), 15, 20 (bottom), 23 (top right), 27, 56 (top), 64–5, 102 (right), 112, 114, 128, 134 (top), 141 (top), 149 (top) Golf Picture Library © Matthew Harris; pages 1, 2 (bottom), 7 (bottom), 8 (bottom), 9 (middle right), 23 (bottom right), 35 (right), 73 Hobbs Golf Collection; page 7 (middle) A. G. Ingram Ltd; pages 39, 48 Inpho; page 74 (top) Kemsley Picture Service; pages 3, 5 (middle), 5 (bottom), 42 (top), 67 (right), 89 (left) Lafayette Photography; page 123 (bottom) David Meehan Photography; pages 6, 19 (bottom) The National Library of Ireland; page 22 Tralee Golf Club; pages 127 (bottom), 130 (top) Northern Ireland Tourist Board; page 44 (bottom) Photographic P. R. Services; pages 8 (top), 11, 16 (top), 30, 32 (bottom), 33 (top), 46 (bottom), 68 (bottom left), 91 (bottom), 131, 150 Quadrillion Publishing Ltd; pages 1 (top), 9 (middle left), 9 (bottom left), 13 (left), 13 (right), 34 (top right), 36 (left), 37 (bottom), 40 (top), 43 (top and bottom), 51, 52, 54 (bottom), 61 (top and bottom), 62 (bottom), 70 (top and bottom), 71 (bottom left), 82, 83, 86 (left), 87 (top), 93 (bottom), 97 (top), 99 (bottom), 100, 101 (right), 104, 105 (top and bottom), 107 (top, middle and bottom), 116, 118, 119 (top), 120 (top and bottom) Phil Sheldon Golf Picture Library, © Phil Sheldon; page 63 (bottom) Joseph Tattan 'Golfshots'; page 20 United States Golf Association.

The publishers have used all efforts to trace copyright-holders and have sought and received permission from each source. However, they will make the usual and appropriate arrangements with any who may have been overlooked inadvertently and who contact hem.

THE ORIGINS OF GOLF IN IRELAND

T HE BEGINNING OF GOLF IN IRELAND is lost in the misty past, every bit as much as the origins of the game itself. Nobody knows for certain where it was first played. Delving into history in search of the game's ancestry has been a favourite and passionate occupation of golf *aficionados* down through the ages. But the deliberations still have more to do with the possible and the probable, rather than the absolute.

Without a definitive milestone, centuries-old conjecture continues in the absorbing debate. Holland has strongest claims on golf's antecedence, regardless of notions that stick-and-ball traditions can similarly be traced in France, Italy and even China.

But Scotland also stands apart, even though its case is founded more on hearsay than on fact.

Yet, if we generally tend towards the lobby proclaiming that the ancient game probably did have Dutch roots, the truth is that Scotland must take the greater acclaim for consolidating and popularising the game.

Cold and aloof as it is ever depicted, St Andrews and its famous Old Course may not necessarily be where the game of golf drew its first breath of life. Yet, there can be no doubt but that hers was the hand that rocked the cradle and hers was the maternal eye that guided the game to its full maturity.

As ever, the caring Old Lady has endured as that doting parent, and the mythology embracing the ancient cobble-stoned town of the Home of Golf and the legend enveloping the great patriarchal Old Tom Morris and his son, Young Tom, ensure its place in the history of golf.

In Ireland we accept that the introduction of golf here was, indeed, a gift from Scotland.

Everything points in that direction.

This fascination with the origins of golf in Ireland, especially those pertaining to its Scottish influence, is fuelled all the more by the background to one Hugh Montgomery.

The belief is that the Honourable Laird of Braidstane, hailing from the west coast of Scotland, had found his way to the Ards Peninsula about 1603. There, in the company of a fellow Scot and free spirit named James Hamilton, they acquired some land.

Montgomery had served time with the Scottish Regiment in Holland, and while there he may well have joined in the local pastime of a game called 'het kolven' or more simply 'kolven'. This is an event featured in innumerable paintings and sketches by old masters that hang in Dutch museums and that are always used as evidence of Holland being the birthplace of the game. The historian Bill Gibson, a man who has done more research on golf in Ireland than anyone, provides a telling insight into the story of golf in Ireland in his

Patriarchal Old Tom Morris.

Young Tom Morris.

The game of Kolven, featured in paintings and sketches and ever used as evidence of Holland being the birthplace of golf.

The promenade at Bray and common on which the first playing of golf in Ireland may have taken place.

Golf at Bray.

book, *Early Irish Golf*, by revealing that the pioneering Montgomery had, as a gesture, built a school at Newtown, 'allowing the scholars a green for recreation at goff, football and archery'. This, concludes Gibson, is the first recorded mention of 'goff', or golf as we came to know it, in Ireland. The year was 1606.

Thereafter, nothing further can be traced on the story of the game in the Newtownards area (until late in the nineteenth century). History records that the locality of the Montgomery plantation, and all its virtues, was to be devastated in the Rebellion of 1641. Indeed, this period also produces the first pictorial reference with a direct Irish golf connotation in the classic depiction of Charles I, while on the golf links at Leith, halting his game to accept from a messenger the news of an Irish rebellion.

While it is in the north of Ireland that the Irish origins of the game may be found, the scales tilt towards the south and, in particular, to the seaside town of Bray in County Wicklow for the discovery of the first verifiable playing of golf in Ireland about 1762.

Today, the townland of Bray is a bustling holiday resort and a rapidly expanding urban district south of Dublin, and while there is no argument that the record books outline the Royal Belfast Golf Club as the oldest in the country, it seems that the old fishing village of Bray may have preceded all.

Among its frayed and faded pages, a newspaper journal of the day carries the critically informative information: 'The Goff club meet to dine at the house of Mr Charles Moran at Bray on Thursday, the 28th October, 1762 at half an hour after three o'clock —, Elias de Butts, Esq in the Chair.'

This is accepted as the first evidence of a 'goff' or golf club in Ireland. And de Butts and, by association, Moran take the distinction of being regarded as Ireland's first known golf club members! By all accounts the members of the (Bray) Goff Club played on a common piece of land by the seashore. The area can now be identified as that adjacent to the popular sea front promenade.

If the absence of more detailed evidence restricts the formal identification of Bray as Ireland's first club, historians are similarly frustrated at the absence of documentation to confirm that the Curragh Club in County Kildare might also, in fact, have been the first established club in Ireland.

In the case of the Curragh, its official listing shows 1883 as the year of its institution. Yet, encompassed in a quaint old story of a gutta percha ball is evidence that golf was played on the Curragh, near Donnelly's Hollow, as far back as 1852.

The story is that an old gutty ball was once discovered, with a label attached bearing the clear inscription: 'Straffan, Co. Kildare. This ball was played by me in a match with the late Alexander Love on the Links, near Donnelly's Hollow, Curragh, on July 15th, 1885.' It was signed by Mr David Ritchie, a Scot, which is itself significant. He had come to live in Ireland in 1851 as a member of the Royal Musselburgh Club, and it was he who laid out the course on the Curragh.

David Ritchie, a pioneering Scot, who migrated to Ireland in 1851 and laid out a golf course at the Curragh.

Given that there still is an absence of hard historical evidence, what of the claims that golf was Gaelic in origin? The notion is based on a contention by Rev. Alphonsus Ryan, one time captain of the Hermitage Club in west Dublin, and who it was said put as much study into his research as did any of the other experts who have tried to solve the mystery.

The worthy Fr Ryan based his submission on the fact that the word 'stymie' (once an integral part of the game whereby a player's ball could wilfully be played in a manner so as to block an opponent's line to the hole) is Gaelic in origin.

Further, he suggested that the ancient wooden implements of the game and the way it is played, i.e. grip, stance, swing and method of striking are similar to the caman (hurley) and to the way the national game of hurling is played.

Of course, it's all a little bit far fetched. Yet, set against the documentation outlined by Marcus de Burca in his book, *The GAA: A History of the Gaelic Athletic Association*, it makes you think. Underlining the fact that the earliest references to hurling come from the very dawn of civilisation in Ireland, he documents how the national game has been a distinctively Irish pastime for at least 2,000 years.

Camanacht (or 'commoning' in English) was essentially played in the northern half of Ireland in wintertime with a slender stick and a hard ball, and was a form of ground hurling in which the ball was not lifted into the hand. History records how the parliament sitting in Kilkenny in 1367 argued that too much game-playing led to neglect of military service, stipulated that 'the land of Ireland' should not be used for 'the plays . . . men call horlings [sic] with great sticks upon the ground'.

Shortly after this, Archbishop Colton of Armagh threatened excommunication for Catholics who played the 'reprehensible' game of hurling, since it led to 'mortal sins, beatings and . . . homicides'.

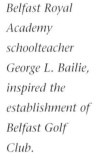

Belfast Royal Academy schoolteacher George L. Bailie, inspired the establishment of Belfast Golf Club.

Thomas Sinclair, returned from Scotland in 1881, bitten by the golfing bug.

However, the ball and its label were either lost, stolen or destroyed by fire, having been presented on its discovery to the Royal Dublin Club.

Once again, this was a frustrating case of priceless golfing memorabilia failing to survive and sustain critical proof of the early era in Irish golf history.

There was also seen to be a strong Scottish influence behind the steps taken in Belfast one morning in October 1881, heralding the modern era of Irish golf. A Mr Thomas Sinclair, later to become the Right Honourable, returned from a holiday in Scotland bitten by the golfing bug and in search of a Mr George Bailie, a native of Musselburgh, who was in Ireland as a member of the teaching staff at the Belfast Royal Academy School.

Mr Bailie had already earned a reputation as a golfer and when he jumped at the proposition made by the enthusiastic Mr Sinclair, it was only a matter of weeks before the Belfast Club was formed. From this historic landmark, the formal playing and club establishment of golf in Ireland gathered momentum.

All the while, the game was winning appeal in Scotland and England, so that visitors to Ireland who already played the game accelerated its growth throughout the country, even though club centenary histories are littered with stories of how clubs were formed, ceased to operate for whatever reason, only to be re-established at a later date.

Soon a band of dedicated golfers was to take control of developments and once moves were initiated to form a national union, the game spread rapidly. According to William A. Menton, former secretary of the Golfing Union of Ireland, the inspiration leading to the founding of the game's first union is not quite clear. It may have been at a summer meeting of the County Club at Portrush in June 1891 when the establishment of an Irish championship was discussed. Menton does tell us that it was at the autumn meeting of the County Down

Not everyone was enamoured at the first sight of organised golf in Dublin in the mid-1880s.

The 'Red Loonies' was how advocates were described as they pursued their new-found passion on the twelve holes that were laid out in the Phoenix Park near the Magazine Fort.

By obligation the members of the Dublin Golf Club wore a red coat and knickerbockers by way of a warning signal to passers-by, thus being referred to as the 'Red Loonies'.

Letter from George Combe to Royal and Ancient Club, dated 20 November 1891, confirming the formation of a Golfing Union of Ireland and requesting 'a copy of the rules governing your Championship meeting, so that we may have some basis to go on in arranging ours'.

Club on 26 September 1891 that the idea of a union was formally suggested, probably by Thomas Gilroy. Just over two weeks later, on 12 October, a meeting was held in the Northern Counties Railway Hotel, Portrush, for the purpose of forming a Golfing Union and of establishing an Irish Championship meeting.

The attendance at this meeting included: Captain James L. McCalmont (Captain, Royal Belfast) who was elected chairman, John S. Alexander and John Patrick (County Down), Hugh Adair (Killymoon), William H. Mann (Aughnacloy), John Kinley and Dr Charles L. Magill (Dungannon) and Hugh C. Kelly (County).

The first resolution to be adopted was: 'That it is desirable to establish a Golfing Union, consisting of representatives of all Golf Clubs in Ireland.' It was also agreed that the immediate objects of the Union would be:

- to fix the dates of all competitions to avoid clashing;
- to consider the advisability of organising an Irish Championship meeting;
- to adopt some fixed principle of handicapping;
- to treat with the different railway companies with a view to obtaining railway facilities for golfers; and
- generally to consider such matters as may be for the advancement of golf in Ireland.

Captain James M. McCalmot M.P. who chaired the meeting in October 1891 'for the purpose of forming a Golfing Union and of establishing an Irish Championship meeting'.

George Combe, first honorary secretary of the Golfing Union of Ireland, 1891 to 1899.

Fashionable Grafton Street, one of Dublin's principal shopping areas, an old army fort in the city's Phoenix Park, and Captain William Bligh of the *Bounty* seem an unlikely combination with reference to golf. Yet, strange as it appears, all three are at the core of the early development of golf and the formation of the Royal Dublin Club, the longest established in Dublin and the first club in Ireland to have an eighteen hole course.

The Scottish influence on the development of the game in Ireland is once more illustrated, as it was the Scottish-born John Lumsden, a banker who had come to take up a post in Dublin, who was the principal behind the formation of the Dublin Golf Club in 1885 at 19 Grafton Street, Dublin. Queen Victoria approved the royal patronage seven years later.

The club was first sited in the Phoenix Park on nine holes around the Magazine Fort. It was developed by soldiers of the Scottish regiments; but as the discerning players of the day had a preference for links rather than parkland underfoot, they moved to an area near Sutton before it, in turn, proved inadequate to the needs and demands, and the club found its present home on the Bull Wall.

This location can be partly attributed to William Bligh! When Fletcher Christian and his fellow mutineeers consigned Bligh to the mercy of the ocean from the *Bounty* in 1789 with no regard for his prospect of survival, little could it have been envisaged that Bligh would have a hand in the formation of one of Ireland's best-known courses, famous also for the fact that it is built on the wildlife preserve of Bull Island, within a fifteen minute bus ride from the centre of a capital city.

Grafton Street.

Captain Bligh was among those invited, around 1800, to make suggestions to the Port of Dublin Authority on how best to provide shipping with a safe, straight and deep approach on the River Liffey into the heart of Dublin. The information he submitted was helpful when the proposal for a breakwater extending from Dollymount was implemented.

The silting up that led to the formation of the Bull Wall resulted in a sandbank being created from which the island grew and produced a rich crop of bent and red fescue grass that to this day yields the base for the greens and fairways of the links course.

The Bull Island has world recognition as a sanctuary for birds, some of which travel from Arctic Canada and Siberia. The island was declared a UNESCO Biosphere Reserve in 1981. There is always birdlife to be seen, but the most numerous visitors are the brent geese. They fly 3,000 miles from Arctic Canada via Iceland and Greenland. Good feeding is essential as they must store up energy for the return flight.

As well as brent geese, teal, curlew, oyster-catcher and shelduck, the island is also famous for its hares.

At an adjourned meeting which had been fixed for 13 November at the Royal Hotel, Belfast, the resolution, 'That the Golfing Union be and is hereby established', was formally submitted and passed.

All the while, of course, clubs were being founded all over Ireland, and the fact that the pioneers of the Union were seen to achieve their stated objective to make the game more popular was illustrated in the statistic that in the eight years between 1892 and 1900, as many as ninety-seven clubs were established.

The final decade of the nineteenth century can be referred to as the golden period in Irish golf, and it is exemplified by an article in the *Belfast Newsletter* of 10 August 1896:

> That the Royal and Ancient game has taken a firm and permanent hold on this country is plainly evidenced by the frequency with which new links are being opened in different parts. With the natural advantages which we are fortunate in possessing in this country, it would be ungrateful did we not exercise to the full our opportunities for developing to the utmost a game which is adapted to indulgence by both sexes, and to the young and old in each.

The pace was helped by the advent of national and open competition, spawning the first home-bred heroes of the game and, in tandem, attracting into the country many of the players now revered as the legends of old.

Furthermore, the spread of the game was encouraged by Arthur J. Balfour, the Chief Secretary for Ireland. An enthusiastic player himself, he became a captain of the Royal and Ancient at St Andrews.

Proof that ladies were as attracted to this irresistible pastime as the gentlemen can be gauged by the formation of the Irish Ladies' Golf Union in 1893 — the first of its kind in the game. It was followed one year later in 1894 by the United States Golf Association, in 1895 by the Welsh Golfing Union, in 1920 by the Scottish Golf Union and in 1924 by the English Golf Union.

The Aughnacloy putter, first competed for in 1889 and still a treasure of Dungannon Golf Club.

Long nosed woods.

Alexander Stuart, winner of the inaugural Irish Amateur Open Championship in 1892.

Early gutta percha balls and featheries.

1881: Kinnegar, Holywood, County Down — the birthplace of Royal Belfast Golf Club.

The Golfing Union of Ireland became the first national controlling body of golf in the world when it was founded in 1891.

That golf in Ireland was being administered on a national level before any other nation is further illustrated by the statistic that the United States Golf Association came into existence in 1894, followed by the Welsh Golfing Union in 1895, the Scottish Golf Union in 1920 and the English Golf Union in 1924.

Writing in *The Irish Ladies' Golf Union: An Illustrated Centenary History (1893–1993)*, Dermot Gilleece says: 'On an autumn day in 1887, a remarkably far-sighted woman, Miss C. E. McGee, travelled to Kinnegar, Holywood, County Down, on a rather curious mission. The trip was made at the invitation of a Dr Collier, who was convinced she would be intrigued by the sight of a very rare species. A lady golfer!'

Sometime later, in a letter to her friend, Miss Leah Garratt, Miss McGee wrote that she had been introduced to the lady golfer who 'inspired me with a wish to play the game'. The golfer in question was the wife of a Captain Wright of the Scottish Light Infantry, and that inspirational incident would become a key element in the founding of the Irish Ladies' Golf Union.

In the history of Royal Belfast Golf Club we are informed that her enjoyment of golf led Miss McGee to discusss with a fellow enthusiast the possibility of forming a ladies' golf club. And so it began.

Following the lead of the Holywood ladies, other clubs, notably Killymoon, Newcastle, Portrush, Dungannon and Belmont, encouraged women to take up the game at a time when, interestingly, golf was played mostly in winter, the highlight being an annual match against the men on Boxing Day.

The driving force behind the involvement and spread of women's golf in Ireland remained the redoubtable Miss McGee, and it was wholly in keeping with her enthusiasm that she found the support for her long-cherished objective that a Union be formed.

Early 20th-century rake iron.

From times past — mid-iron, jigger, push iron and anti shank niblicks.

And so it came to pass on Friday, 15 December 1893, in the Girls' Friendly Society Lodge, Belfast, that a meeting was held to form an Irish Ladies' Golf Union. Clubs in attendance were Royal Belfast (to which Miss McGee was attached), Royal County, Portrush and Dungannon.

Among the resolutions passed were:

1. That in the interest of golf in Ireland, it is desirable that a Union of the Irish Ladies' Golf Clubs be and is hereby formed and shall be called The Irish Ladies' Golf Union.
2. That an annual Championship meeting be held and that the first meeting be held at Carnalea in April, 1894, at Portrush in 1895 and at Newcastle in 1896.

And so golf in Ireland was now formally organised.

Early 19th century 'Rut' iron . . . when a golfer of the 1830s found his expensive feathery ball in a rut made by a carriage wheel etc. he would use this type of club to 'dig' his ball out rather than risk damaging it with a wooden club. The neck of the club was always approximately five inches long so as to absorb the shock of such a steep blow.

THE "UNIVERSAL" GOLF BAG CARRIER.

Price: 3/6

Patent No. 18,390.

Special Advantages:

Can be attached to any Cycle in one minute and will carry any Golf Bag.

Does not interfere with the rider or in any way alter steering or balance of machine.

Trade Supplied by . . .

F. COLLINS (Professional), Llandudno Golf Club, LLANDUDNO.

ESTABLISHED 1835.

Appointed by Engineers to His Majesty

Royal Warrant, Horticultural King Edward VII.

GREEN'S GOLF MOWER,

fitted with Shafts, Driver's Seat, and Foot Rest.

The BEST and most EFFECTIVE Machine for GOLF LINKS on the Market.

THOMAS GREEN & SON, Ltd., SMITHFIELD IRON WORKS, LEEDS; and Surrey Works, Blackfriars Rd., London. Telegraphic Addresses: "SMITHFIELD, LEEDS"; "SURREY WORKS, LONDON."

☞ Send for Illustrated Price List (Free). ☜

Lady golfers, circa 1893.

THE DEVELOPMENT OF GOLF CLUBS IN IRELAND

THOSE ESTABLISHED BETWEEN 1890 AND 1900:

1881 Royal Belfast (originally Belfast) affiliated to the Golfing Union in 1891.

1883 Curragh (originally Curragh, then Royal Curragh) (1898); Fota Island (Co. Cork).

1885 Royal Dublin (originally Dublin) (1892).

1886 Mornington (Co. Meath).

1888 Aughnacloy (Co. Tyrone); Cork (1900); Royal Portrush (originally County Antrim, County, Royal County) (1891).

1889 Killymoon (1891); Queen's County Heath (Queen's County, now County Laois); Royal County Down (originally County Down) (1891).

1890 Ballycastle (1891); Bushfoot (1906); Dublin Scottish (Sutton, Co. Dublin); Dungannon (1891); Shane's Park (Rondalstown, Co. Antrim) (1893); The Island (1901).

1891 Belmont (Garnerville, Co. Down); Limerick (1909); Lisburn (Co. Antrim) (1894); North West (originally Buncrana) (1891); Omagh (originally Tyrone, Co. Tyrone); Portsalon (1891); Rushbrook (Co. Cork) (1905); Thomastown (Co. Kilkenny) (1923).

1892 Athlone (originally Athlone Garrison) (1899); County Louth (1895); Greencastle (1896); Lahinch (1897); Lismore (Co. Waterford); Malahide (1905); Mallow (1948); Nenagh (1911); Newry, Rostrevor (1894).

1893 Ballybunion (1909); Bandon (1911); Birr (originally King's County and Ormond, Parsonstown) (1912); County Armagh (1894); Fermoy (1905); Foxrock (1894); Killarney (1909); Lurgan (1894); Ormeau (1894); Otway (1893); Roscrea (originally Mill Park) (1896); Stillorgan, Warrenpoint (1894).

1894 Ballinasloe (1911), Banagher (Taylor's Cross, King's County, now Co. Offaly); Bundoran (1895); Cookstown (Co. Cavan) (1899); County Sligo (1902); Dublin University (1896); Greenisland (1896); Larne (1895); Mullingar (originally County Westmeath) (1905); Newborough (Co. Wexford); Portadown (1902); Portmarnock (1895); Portstewart (1895); Tramore (originally Waterford and Tramore) (1905).

1895 Abbeyleix (1905); Ballinrobe (1902); Blackrock (Rochestown, Co. Cork); Clonakilty (1916); County Monaghan (1907); Dooks (originally Glenbeigh Dooks, then Glenbeigh, Caragh and Dooks) (1903); Dromore (Co. Down); Galway (1899); Greystones (1897); Knock (1896); Malone (1895); Massereene (1896); Rosapenna (1898).

1896 Ardfert (Co. Kerry); Ardglass (1900); Coleraine; Dufferin (Killyleagh, Co. Down); Enniskillen (1911); Greenore (1896); Helen's Bay (1906); Kilkee (1908); Kilkenny (1910); Magilligan (Co. Derry); Naas (originally County Kildare) (1907); Saintfield (Rowallane, Co. Down); Spanish Point (originally West Clare) (1915); Sutton (originally Sutton Yacht and Boat Club) (1899); Tipperary (1906); Toome (Co. Antrim); Trabolgan (Co. Cork); Tralee (1907); Tullamore (1899).

1897 Bray (1899); Carrick (Co. Donegal); Corick (Clogher, Co. Tyrone); Courtmacsherry (Co. Cork); Derrynane (Co. Kerry); Ennis Old; Kinsale; Lucan (originally Moore of Meath) (1905); Muskerry (1910); Newmarket (Co. Cork); Scrabo Old (Co. Down); Woodenbridge (1899); Youghal (1912).

1898 Ardara (Co. Donegal); Newport (Co. Tipperary); Trim (originally the Royal Meath) (1904).

1899 Carlow (originally Leinster) (1901); Donaghadee (1900); Garron Tower (Co. Antrim); Rathfarnham (1900).

1900 Adare Manor (originally Adare) (1932); Berehaven (Co. Cork) (1939); Carrickmines (1901); Castlerock (1902); County Longford (1910); Killaloe (Co. Clare); Moate (1925).

IRELAND'S GREAT COURSES

T HERE IS NO DOUBT BUT THAT IRELAND IS BLESSED with regard to the number and quality of its golf courses. Be they big, rolling championship links or leafy, parkland courses, there is always a great variety from which to choose.

In any discussion on great golf courses of the world, you will inevitably hear the claims being put forward of Ballybunion, Portmarnock, Royal Portrush, Royal County Down, Lahinch, Rosses Point, Royal Dublin and Killarney. And, in every instance, the argument stands up.

Yet to restrict the choice to this hardy roll of honour is to understate vastly the golfing amenities of Ireland. Account must also be taken (among others) of Tralee, Waterville, Connemara, Westport and Donegal, all relatively new courses but of sufficient quality to vie with the longer-established ones.

Imposing clubhouse facilities overlook Ballybunion's 18th green.

Take note, also, that the admirable Jack Nicklaus has given his signature to the greatly acclaimed new course on the woodland Mount Juliet estate in County Kilkenny, while Arnold Palmer has created the quite fantastic Kildare Golf and Country Club, more generally known as the K Club. These courses were inspired by successful businessmen wishing to give Ireland a standard of golf not previously available. The endeavours of Tim Mahony at Mount Juliet and Michael Smurfit at the K Club have set an example that many have tried to emulate.

They have a hard act to follow, for Irish golf course architecture is steeped in the very best traditions.

Unique Royal Portrush — the original work of Harry Colt.

11

*Sunset on the 17th . . .
an intrepid threeball
set for home before
darkness consumes
famous Ballybunion.*

*From times long past:
canvas bag and hickory
clubs, original
possessions of
Ballybunion club
stalwart John Macauley.*

Recall the skilled hand of immortal Old Tom Morris, of the unique Harry Vardon, of James Braid, Harry Colt, Willie and Mungo Park from that outstanding and innovative Musselburgh family, of the eccentric Tom Simpson and of Alister Mackenzie, the man who spurned a medical career so that he could indulge his passion for golf course design and whose everlasting epitaph is that he collaborated in the creation of Augusta in association with the great Bobby Jones.

Pay equal homage to the work of Ireland's own Eddie Hackett whose ample portfolio takes account of Waterville, Donegal, Enniscrone and Connemara. It is not far wide of the mark to say that there is hardly a golf course of worth in the country that has not at some stage consulted Ireland's most prolific golf course improver and designer.

It was Robert Trent Jones, surely the *world's* most prolific golf course architect, who was moved to enthuse that the land on which he has constructed the second eighteen holes at Ballybunion, is quite simply 'the finest natural golfing territory I have seen'. Down the road at Barrow, just outside the town of Tralee, Arnold Palmer's first ever design in Ireland moved him to declare: 'I am happy we have one of the world's greatest links here.'

It is hardly surprising that he should be so inspired. The site across which the Tralee course spreads itself is unquestionably one of the most scenic to be found. It is a

Classic pose graphically illustrating the trend-setting overlapping grip of Harry Vardon, renowned six times British Open champion, who had a huge influence on early Irish golf course design.

stunningly beautiful site overlooking the golden spread of Banna Strand, chosen for its location during the making of David Lean's acclaimed film, *Ryan's Daughter*. To play along the par five 11th called Palmer's Peak, which offers panoramic views of the Dingle Peninsula, is enough to take your breath away.

At Tralee you will further savour something out of the ordinary when negotiating the narrow par four 4th hole known as Cúchulainn's Table, when playing the 5th hole named after St Brendan the Navigator, whose famous voyage is depicted in the club badge, and when faced with the daunting challenge of the 190 yards carry downhill to the 16th green. This hole is called Shipwreck, with good reason; an over robust shot will carry over the adjacent clifftop into the sea amid the ruins of many old sailing disasters.

Of the refurbished Waterville, Sam Snead said: 'A beautiful monster is born!' Set as a centrepiece on the famous Ring of Kerry, the one-time holiday haunt of Charlie Chaplin and his family is now as much a golfing mecca as it is a fishing and seaside holiday resort. Established by the Irish-American John A. Mulcahy, this is

The taciturn James Braid, tall and aloof and ever identifiable by his distinctive walrus moustache, gave Ireland the rolling parkland of Bangor, the ambience of leafy Newlands, the uniqueness of Grange, the serene setting at Mullingar and Tullamore, the tilting terrain at Waterford, the special flavour of Howth and the blend of links and parkland at Whitehead.

one of the great creations of Eddie Hackett, readily acclaimed by all who make the trek to one of the most beautiful corners of Ireland. Along with Snead, fellow Americans Raymond Floyd ('Waterville has some of the finest links holes I have ever played') and Tom Watson ('Waterville possesses the best par three holes I have ever encountered on the same golf course') have been vociferous in their praise.

Among its many features, two par three holes, the 12th and the 17th, stand apart. The 12th of roughly 200 yards is

Harold Colt, whose design concepts in Ireland were greatly influenced by what he admired at St Andrews.

known as the Mass Hole as a reminder of Penal times when local inhabitants were obliged to celebrate their Catholic religion, for fear of persecution, within the concealed hollow that now forms the carry from tee to green.

Equally, the 17th will fill you with terror, with respect and (possibly) with fulfilment. The tee stands 250 feet above sea level. It is called Mulcahy's Peak. It was there that John Mulcahy used to stand, inspired by the majestic panorama, as he plotted the course in his mind's eye. He insisted that a tee be placed there so that all who play Waterville

A hole that will exhilarate and terrify, is how legendary Harry Vardon described the 9th at Royal County Down, one of the most photographed holes in golf. A quite superb design, demanding at least two great shots, its virtue is further illuminated by its scenic splendour. Standing on top of the heather-strewn hill over which the drive is aimed, you are captivated by the sight of the majestic Mourne Mountains quite literally sweeping down to the sea by the sandy expanse of Dundrum Bay.

Steering a course back towards the imposing clubhouse and aiming 'on the spire' of the distinctive red-bricked Slieve Donard Hotel, a high and long drive must carry over the brow of the hill, tumbling down to a fairway 80 feet below. That is only half the battle; the remainder demands that the eye of the needle must also be threaded to avoid casualty among the spectacular bunkers.

Famed 9th fairway at Royal County Down and a time-honoured view of Dundrum Bay, the Mountains of Mourne and the distinctive red-bricked Slieve Donard Hotel.

will depart with a memory of the unique setting. The tee shot is roughly 190 yards. The ball must traverse uncharted dunes described as 'an emerald oasis amidst a jungle of nature's own terrain'. Be prepared to tee up again and hit three!

The late distinguished golf writer, Peter Dobereiner, advised golfers: 'They may not call themselves true believers until they have made a pilgrimage to Ireland. I have to say that Robert Louis Stevenson was wrong when he said the Monterey Peninsula in California was the finest conjunction of land and sea this earth has to offer as a spectacle. The south-west corner of Ireland is in a different class.'

The legendary Herbert Warren Wind, writing in the *New Yorker*, said that Old Ballybunion was 'simply the greatest golf links in the world'. Of neighbouring Killarney, Gene Sarazen said: 'When the wind blows in off the lake, even the best players in the world will be hard pressed to break 80.' And he added: 'Surely, the 18th par three on the O'Mahony's Point course is one of the most memorable holes in the game.'

Killarney, the locals would have you believe, 'is the end result of what the good Lord Almighty can do when He's in a good mood.' It is hard to disagree when you have the choice of playing the lakeside Killeen course hard by Macgillycuddy's Reeks, or the more inland O'Mahony's Point amid the clusters of white and rose-coloured rhododendrons. Now they are to have a third course.

Yet the endless list of fine courses in Ireland is not confined to the more traditionally lauded landmarks. Among the longer-established clubs there are some less-documented venues good enough to be rated among the best there are to be found. In this

Killarney by the lakes (the 10th hole on the Killeen course) locals argue, 'is the end result of what the Lord Almighty can do when He's in a good mood'.

regard, Baltray, Mullingar, The Island, Carlow, Grange and Hermitage, to mention a leading group, stand out.

In Northern Ireland the merits of Royal Portrush, Royal County Down, Portstewart and Castlerock are invariably documented. Not necessarily known on a wider scale are the courses of Belfast itself.

Any discerning golfer would want to sign the visitors' book at Royal Belfast, Ireland's oldest club, or to pay a call to the Balmoral Club where Fred Daly, Ireland's only British

The peninsula at Portmarnock was pretty much uncharted territory in 1893 when, purely out of curiosity, George Ross, a Dublin solicitor, and his Scottish companion, W. C. Pickeman, who was an insurance broker, rowed across the estuary from Sutton.

They shared an interest in golf and had wondered about the potential of the isolated land of Portmarnock. To their delight, they indeed found the making of a good golf course amidst a haven whose inhabitants and surroundings seemed strangely but contentedly remote from the mainland, just a stone's throw away.

Fortunately, the landowner John Jameson, one of the distilling family, was a golfing enthusiast and readily signed a twenty-five year lease 'on most moderate terms'. The first clubhouse was an outhouse belonging to a local resident, Maggie Leonard, and adjoining her cottage. A formal opening took place on St Stephen's Day in 1894.

George Ross marked the opening by hitting the first official shot. The driver he used remains a treasured memento in the clubhouse to this day.

Portmarnock's signature 15th hole by the Irish Sea and described by Ben Crenshaw as 'one of the greatest short holes on earth'.

Portmarnock began modestly with nine holes laid out by Pickeman, with Mungo Park as greens architect. Two years later the second nine holes were opened.

But it was not all sweetness for the pioneers of Portmarnock. They had to contend with a big hazard in Maggie Leonard — and her cow!

Maggie's thatched cottage nestled behind the 1st green and she had a cow remarkable for her appetite for golf balls, hundreds of which she devoured. One unnamed member of the club gave Maggie a half ton of the best coal each winter; in return he received most of the lost balls.

There was also the problem of getting to the course. There were few motor cars in those early days and transport from Dublin was by rail to Sutton, by road to Baldoyle and by sea to the clubhouse. Many are the stories of wettings and near drownings in the crossing of the strip of sea made either by boat or by side car, depending on the state of the tide.

This historic picture hangs in the members' bar at Portmarnock, depicting a group on the 5th hole playing in the Captain's match on the day the links was formally opened, St Stephen's Day, 1894.

THE HOME GREEN, ROSAPENNA.

R. WELCH.

Rosapenna — a links steeped in the best traditions and offering an insight into the architectural mind of Old Tom Morris.

Former days when competition on the links at Rosapenna was a regular feature.

Rosses Point: 'From the 5th tee, you look down the side of a cliff to a breathtaking panorama of holes spreading into the distance below. Mountains on one side, sea on the other, all add to the wild grandeur of the majestic rolling surroundings. I had heard a lot about Ballybunion, Tralee, Connemara and Lahinch, but Rosses Point stands right at the very top of the list of Irish golf courses and it is one that more people should discover.' (Peter Alliss)

Ballybunion: 'After playing Ballybunion for the first time, a man would think that the game of golf originated here. Ballybunion is a course on which many golf architects should live and play before they build golf courses. I consider it the true test of golf.'
(Tom Watson)

Open winner, was in residence for so long and where there is still lovingly preserved in a corner of the lounge bar a monument to their most famous member. The lovely Malone and the rolling nature of its fairways encircling a great lake filled with trout is another excellent venue. So too is Belvoir Park, with five par threes, and the enviable siting of a clubhouse from which almost every hole can be viewed, each and every one a gem. But then you need hardly be surprised, as the late and legendary Henry Longhurst wrote: 'In Ireland, they have the greatest golf courses in the world, not only in layout and design, also in scenery and atmosphere and that indefinable something which makes you relive again and again the day you played there.'

The life-blood of golf in Ireland traces its origins to a gift of providence, and how man improved on that blessing. The tone is established in the case of the mighty Royal County Down at Newcastle in its majestic setting at the foot of the dramatically scenic Mourne Mountains and by the sandy expanse of Dundrum Bay. It was essentially laid out by Tom Morris and later improved by way of subtle augmentation by Vardon and then by Colt.

When Morris was deputed to carry out his work in 1889, he was obliged to restrict his spending to four guineas. In today's terms that converts to around £240, a far cry from the startling costs and end result of much of our own generation's contribution to the golf course concept.

The same prominent names are repeated constantly when researching golf course design in Ireland. For example, the skills of patriarchal Old Tom Morris are evident across the fescued fairways at Ballybunion, Royal Portrush, Lahinch and Rosapenna.

The story of how Rosapenna in County Donegal came into being provides an insight into the mind of Morris and architectural thinking in Ireland over a century ago. It is said that his 'practised eye was at once struck by the adaptability of the ground to the requirements of the game and with his prophetic instinct he predicted before long — that redcoats would be seen driving the gutta over its fine slopes'.

Railways have always been an integral part of golfing life in Ireland. Ever since, at the inaugural meeting to form the Golfing Union of Ireland in 1891, a resolution was passed 'to treat with the different railway companies with a view to obtaining railway facilities for golfers', the railways have helped to popularise the game.

At the time, it was almost an exception for golf links to be laid out unless within easy reach of a railway halting.

Portrush and Newcastle were targeted by the astute Joseph Tatlow, the enterprising manager of the old Belfast and County Down Railway, as a means of enticing more people to use his service.

The Great Southern and Western Railways followed suit and special concessions were offered to golfers who wished to travel on the West Clare Railway line, immortalised in the lyrics of Percy French, to the Atlantic village of Lahinch.

Golf Links Hotel, Lahinch, Co. Clare.

Perhaps the most unusual railway-golfing connection of them all was the one called after a man with the melodious sounding name of Charles Françoise Marie-Thérèse Lartigue. Running on a monorail between Listowel and Ballybunion, odd, indeed, was the sight of golfers disgorging from the steam-powered, apparently wheel-less locomotive, with the carriages straddled on either side of a single centre rail from an axle on which was mounted a flanged centre and hidden wheel.

It was said that the Lartigue 'gave the impression of two hampers of turf strung across a donkey's back', but the connection into Ballybunion was vital to the formative growth of the locale that went on to claim world renown.

The West Clare Railway line, immortalised in the lyrics of Percy French, arriving in the Atlantic village of Lahinch.

The unusual Lartigue monorail which helped popularise the game of golf.

Eccentric Tom Simpson who travelled around Ireland in a Rolls Royce accompanied by his friend, the accomplished Molly Gourlay.

Subsequently, Braid and Vardon were invited to lend their touch (Eddie Hackett more recently provided some updating brushwork), thus enhancing further the reputation of a splendid course.

Similarly, Ballybunion shows the touches of many a deft architectural hand. The first design features were supplied by Morris during the club's early years, dating back to 1891. Later, the golf writer, Lionel Hewson, was asked to clean up the overgrowth and restore what work Morris had done. By 1927 Hewson had built an additional nine holes. Then came the

County Louth. ....•

eccentric Tom Simpson who travelled about in a Rolls Royce accompanied by his friend, the noted lady golfer of the time, Molly Gourlay, working as a team. The Simpson-Gourlay partnership completed some updating in time for the club to host the Irish Ladies' Championship in 1932 and these features remained intact until Ballybunion requested Tom Watson to carry out some further work in 1995/96.

So impressed were others by the work of Simpson at Ballybunion that the anxious committees at County Louth and Carlow also recruited the services of the architect who had already improved such major British courses as Sunningdale, Royal Porthcawl and Muirfield. Simpson's approach to design coupled the theory that golf was only seen at its best when there is as much necessity for brainwork as for physical endeavour, along with his insistence that no two greens should be alike. Thus his contribution to Carlow, Ballybunion and Baltray is evident.

At Ballybunion a warm and friendly relationship had been established with Tom Watson ever since the American fell in love with the place and established the custom of playing the links in preparation for his British Open forays (which he has won on five occasions). Essentially, Watson's contribution has had to do with bunkering, notably at the 4th, 5th and 16th holes. Somewhat controversially, he has taken out some mounding to open up a view off the 10th tee, heading back down towards the sea; but at the 18th, often criticised for its outdated blind approach to the green, he has been lauded for the decision to cut out a saddle in the raised ground fronting the putting area, so that now at least a glimpse of the flagstick can be seen.

Golf *as Gaelige* . . . with the 19th hole situated in Ireland's only thatched clubhouse, replete with open turf fire.

The off-course attraction helps to underline the unusual nature of Golfmara, a quaint little nine hole course situated on the brink of the Atlantic Ocean in the heart of the Connemara Gaeltacht.

All the virtues of golf in the ruggedly beautiful west of Ireland are captured at this unique island course which is joined to the mainland by a causeway at Bealadangan, a most inviting place to play, especially for the beginner.

THE IRISH DUNLOP COMPANY LIMITED.

TELEGRAPHIC ADDRESS:
"PNEUMATIC, DUBLIN."

TELEPHONE:
DUBLIN 76711 (5 LINES).

DIRECTORS
SIR J. G. BEHARRELL, D.S.O. CHAIRMAN.
J. M. CARROLL.
D. L. DALY.
R. C. FLANAGAN.
H. E. GUINNESS.
H. L. KENWARD.
B. J. O'DONNELL.
D. TELFORD, F.C.A.

REF. D. 54.

REGISTERED OFFICES:
DUNLOP HOUSE,
LOWER ABBEY STREET,
DUBLIN, C.8.

7th May, 1942.

The Secretary,
Ballybunion Golf Club,
Ballybunion,
CO. KERRY.

Dear Sir,

    As an emergency war measure and in order to preserve the game, we have decided to re-cover old golf balls of all makes. The ball will be marked R.M. (as an abbreviation for the word remould) and will be numbered 1-6.

    We shall be pleased to receive from you old golf balls for re-covering which should be sent to The Irish Dunlop Co.Ltd., Marina Works, Cork, carriage paid, in lots of not less than 6 dozen. Your name should appear on the outside of the package and the quantities of balls given on a slip inside the package.

    Balls not suitable for remoulding will be scrapped and you will be advised of the number put in hand for remoulding. Of this number a small percentage may fail in the manufacturing process and the total delivery to you of re-covered balls will be reduced accordingly.

    The trade price for re-covering will be 12/- per dozen and the balls will be returned to you, carriage paid.

    We hope that this service will be of assistance to you.

Yours faithfully,
FOR THE IRISH DUNLOP CO. LTD.,

Emergency war measure.

Splendid vista of
Ballyliffen Old, 5th
hole, and invitingly
beyond.

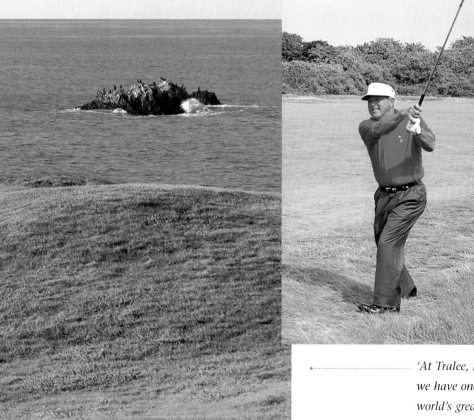

'At Tralee, I am happy
we have one of the
world's greatest links.'
— Arnold Palmer

The taciturn James Braid, tall and aloof and ever identifiable by his distinctive walrus moustache, also gave much to Ireland. Among his treasured gifts are the rolling parkland of Bangor and the tremendous holes of links quality, toughened so much by wind off the Irish Sea, at Kirkistown, both in County Down; the ambience of leafy Newlands and the uniqueness of Grange in Dublin; the serene setting amid the famed old oak at Mullingar and at nearby Tullamore; the tilting terrain at Waterford; the special flavour of Howth; and the blend of seaside and parkland at Whitehead on the Antrim coastline.

The special flavour of Mullingar.

Grange, one of Ireland's better yet largely unsung courses, is a monument to the canny old Scot who endorsed the curiosity of starting with successive par threes — a notion of the original architect, Tom Hood.

At Howth, set so picturesquely atop the hill overlooking Dublin Bay, legend has it that Braid 'got lost in the gorse' as he walked a boggy overgrown area when asked to extend the course to eighteen holes in 1926. It was on Braid's advice that the 'Tank' was built between the 7th and 12th holes, acting as a

reservoir into which the upper part of the lovely north Dublin suburban course drains. For his consultation Braid was paid 28 guineas (or just over £1,000 at today's values)!

If in 1936, at Mullingar, the welcoming committee members who met the former British Open champion at the local railway station were startled when this wily old character asked for a hatchet and three dozen wooden pegs before disappearing amid the heath, gorse and scrub to map out the course in one day, they were positively aghast when their architect returned the following year, during a visit to Tullamore, to answer some criticisms.

The committee had complained to him that it was difficult to hold the ball on the elevated green at the par three 2nd hole, whereupon Braid answered the rebuke by borrowing a club and three balls and proceeded to smack them confidently to the green and control them to a halting finish. The hole has to this day remained largely unaltered.

Calamity Corner is the apt description for the 14th at Royal Portrush, one of the most notorious in the game — and with good reason! Two hundred and fifteen yards off the championship tee, or roughly 205 yards from the medal, one of Ireland's most famous par threes is also one of the most severe. Miss on the right and you are dead, perhaps abandoned to the fates of the wild and rough terrain which sweeps down from the cliff-face. The faint hearted may attempt to negotiate a line into the right-hand hollow by the green. Either way there is a thrilling sense of go-for-broke adventure. You will be all the better for this unique golfing experience!

The rolling parkland course of Westport Golf Club, set on the shores of Clew Bay and in the shadow of Croagh Patrick, stands apart for more than the combination of scenery and sporting challenge.

The golfer can also enjoy a game in an environmentally friendly atmosphere of care and consideration for the virtues of wildlife.

The Gibleen is an area of around 27 acres overlooked by the bay windows of the clubhouse and running hard by the 18th fairway. It is conscientiously preserved by the club authorities.

In its wild and wonderful ambience on the western seaboard, Westport Golf Club, amid ample wood, scrubland and briar, is a safe haven for the creatures of the wild.

The experience of a round of golf is therefore made all the more enlightening by the sight of the occasional fox, stoat and badger, or by duck, mallard, widgeon, teal and brent geese.

Towering Croagh Patrick, the imposing backdrop to invigorating Westport.

Braid, Vardon and Taylor formed the great triumvirate which dominated British and Irish golf for almost thirty years before the outbreak of World War I, and Ireland is fortunate also to have an identification with Harry Vardon.

Many would agree that Vardon was the single most important figure in the game's history. His influence on how the club is held and swung, and his achievement in winning six British Opens (a feat that has defied all to this day), earns him his reputation.

The spirit of Harry Vardon may be recalled when you play from the 1st tee on the clifftop at Bundoran, at challenging Delgany, restorative Douglas and at historic Rosapenna.

Recall too the designing skills of Harold Colt. In international terms he was probably the first outstanding golf architect who had not been previously a professional golfer. The law graduate of Cambridge University had a design portfolio that embraced Rye, Sunningdale and Wentworth in England; Pine Valley in New Jersey, USA; the Eden course at St Andrews and Muirfield in Scotland; and Real Club de Pedrena in Spain where Seve Ballesteros learned his golf.

Many of Ireland's golfing jewels are in constant peril from the ravages of the sea.

Around the coastline every winter there is a fretful sense of anticipation as the remorseless pounding of the Atlantic Ocean and the Irish Sea threaten the destruction of Ireland's priceless golfing heirlooms.

Royal Portrush's classic par four 5th hole and the gem of the one-shot 6th hole are in constant danger, and when he said, 'these links are one of the great heritages of golf and must be protected for present and future generations of golfers', Joe Carr was surely speaking on behalf of all of Ireland's exposed courses.

Woodbrook, Rosslare, Tralee, Ballybunion, Lahinch and Donegal are prominent among those waging a constant battle against the destructive evils of coastal erosion.

As a protection, a familiar sight along the shores is the laying of sea-gabions. They take the form of wire baskets layered with stones and laid to defuse the strength of in-rushing waves crashing against a fairway coastline.

Sea-gabions stand fast against the evils of erosion around the coast of Ireland.

In Ireland, Colt was responsible for the remodelling of Royal Dublin after the links had been mutilated during World War I, when it was commandeered for use by the British Army as a rifle range. The land was handed back in a dilapidated state but, with the compensation of a £10,000 gift, the services of Colt were acquired for a major reconstruction. Taking account of its largely flat terrain, Colt's perceptive eye set about establishing a favourable reminiscence of the Old Course at St Andrews. The old, traditional, out-and-back format gives a clue and its praises are ever sung by Christy O'Connor, Snr, Royal Dublin's favourite son.

Associated with the links since 1959, first as club professional and then as tournament ambassador, the virtues cherished by O'Connor have to do with 'the variety of the four par three holes' and also 'when the course plays its true self, the taxing demand it places on long iron shots to the greens'.

After members of the Old Sligo Militia discovered the County Sligo Club at Rosses Point in 1894, Colt was invited to make improvements around 1920, and they have marvelled at his work ever since. The links was laid out with particular sensitivity to the landscape, not least on the tight 10th fairway where the unrivalled panorama takes account of Ben Bulben, and Drumcliffe churchyard where the great Irish poet W. B. Yeats lies.

The parkland course, amid the trees and colourful foliage of Royal Belfast, tilting gently to the scenic southern shore of Belfast Lough is similarly a design standing to the eternal credit of the most eminent English course architect of the day. Colt's labours have seen to it that Royal Belfast has long endured as one of the finest eighteen hole parkland settings, which is entirely fitting, given the historical seniority held by the club as the oldest established in Ireland.

Perceptively, at The Island in north County Dublin they have also preserved much of the work recommended by Harold Hilton. While there is now easier access by road to the links, once reached only by means of a boat journey across the choppy estuary, what has been retained, amid much updating of the links, are many of the names bequeathed by Hilton. Thus nostalgia is heavy in the air as you tread upon the Broadmeadow, the Andes, the Prairie and the Bowl.

If you have the time to so indulge, stop awhile on the 11th fairway. The club's colourful history pays ample respect to the cricket field upon which the immortal W. G. Grace once played. Legend has it that Grace and some friends came to The Island to play golf in a match against the members. Afterwards, there was the suggestion of a 'knock-up' in which Grace was allegedly bowled out first ball.

The classic 8th hole at The European,
named in memory of the great Fred Daly.

The European Club is situated at Brittas Bay, Co. Wicklow, and set classically amid seaside terrain and dune. It is the first major golf links to appear on Ireland's east coast in this century and well matches in quality and challenge Royal County Down, Royal Portrush, Portmarnock and Baltray.

This precious new addition to Ireland's coastal ring of golfing gems is the creation of Pat Ruddy.

A measure of Ruddy's standing in the game and of the merit of what he has set out to achieve with this, surely his most ambitious golfing venture ever undertaken, is that all the giants of the game have warmly endorsed the project.

Players were asked to nominate the type of golf hole by which they would like to be commemorated. Lee Trevino and Gene Sarazen opted for par threes; Tom Watson and Gary Player asked for par fours; and the upshot is a unique commemoration of some of the game's legends that also serves to provide an insight into their golfing minds.

The holes chosen and nominated are as follows:

Billy Casper	12th	par 4
Henry Cotton	15th	par 4
Fred Daly	8th	par 4
Tony Jacklin	13th	par 5
Byron Nelson	18th	par 4
Arnold Palmer	7th	par 4
Gary Player	11th	par 4
Gene Sarazen	14th	par 3
Sam Snead	4th	par 4
Peter Thomson	5th	par 4
Lee Trevino	6th	par 3
Tom Watson	17th	par 4

And a special tribute to a special friend:
Harry Bradshaw — the putting green

A sting in the tale at the European is the unexpected sight of a water hazard fronting the 18th green. Out of character with the best traditions of links courses — yes. Out of place? Decide for yourself. You'll find the debate in full swing at the 19th.

One of the great legends of Irish golf derives from a charming idiosyncrasy to be found at Lahinch, often referred to as the St Andrews of Irish golf.

It concerns the story of the goats, whose outline adorns the club's crest.

They act as an on-site meteorological service, because local folklore has it that if the weather is going to be fine, the goats will be seen grazing contentedly out among the dunes; whereas when the goats sense the approach of rain and wind, they can be seen gathering in search of shelter in the shadow of the clubhouse. Only the foolhardy fail to take heed!

Such is the legend that when the then club secretary, Brud Slattery, failed in his efforts to repair the broken club barometer, in frustration he posted a notice: 'See Goats.' The barometer still hangs in the clubhouse porch!

Of course, at Lahinch they are sensitive, too, that the forefathers of the game bequeathed a memorial that remains sacrosanct. Set against modern architectural trends, aspects of the rolling links to this day defy acceptance when it comes to playing the par five 5th (Klondyke), where the approach must be aimed blindly over a sandhill straddling the fairway, and again when you come to negotiate the incredible par three 6th, known as the Dell. This is also an infuriatingly camouflaged challenge, curiously concealed behind the whitewashed stone atop another mound on a straight line from the tee. These most unusual holes in golf are the legacy of none other than Old Tom Morris.

When Dr Alister Mackenzie was invited in 1927 to suggest alterations to the course, around which the holiday town of Lahinch thrives, he had the good grace to respect the work of Morris.

It would be a sacrilege for any succeeding generation to dare break a bond so lovingly preserved down through the generations by the renowned Brud Slattery, for so long the proud custodian of all that is best at Lahinch.

The exemplary Dr Mackenzie expressed to the locals an awareness that goes a long way towards identifying the very essence of golf in Ireland. 'How frequently have I persuaded patients of mine who were never off my doorstep to take up golf, and how rarely, if ever, have I seen them in my consulting rooms after,' said the good doctor, who had quit his medical practice to pursue a passion for building golf courses.

Lahinch, which became the nineteenth club to join the Union in 1904 and where the 1904 Ladies' Championship was staged.

Waterville presents 'majestic golf in a majestic setting'.

Proud Donegal golf club by the edge of the great Atlantic Ocean — the 10th hole.

Waterville: 'Majestic golf in a majestic setting. The 11th hole has to be one of the most beautiful par fives of them all! The game here is thrill upon thrill with no respite from the first hole to the last. If you can conquer Waterville you can play the game anywhere and in any company.' (Gary Player)

CITY LIBRARY CORK

One of the most curious legends in golf concerns the Hermit's Cell and Wishing Stone at Hermitage Golf Club on the western outskirts of Dublin.

It has been referred to as a curious geological phenomenon, concealed amid the woodland to the right of the 10th hole, also running parallel to the 9th fairway.

Therein lies the hermit's cave, from which it is claimed the club takes its name. Local tradition holds that the ghostly white-robed figure of the Lady Agnes and her lover can be sometimes glimpsed at dawn, moving through the trees reciting the 'Ballad of the Hermit of Lucan':

Within a cave in time of old,
A hermit did abide,
Where Lucan rears its holy fane,
And River Liffey rolls her tide.

And ever in perpetual youth
They haunt the lovely dell,
All safe from foe or mortal ill,
Protected by a spell.

They flutter 'midst the noble limes,
By Liffey's gentle wave,
Which daily shed a solemn gloom,
Upon the foeman's graves.

Close by is the 'lovers' wishing stone' about which there are many stories of the type traditionally associated with wishing and kissing stones around Ireland!

The signature 10th Hole at Hermitage and adjoining woodland concealing the legend of the Hermit's Cell and Wishing Stone.

Enniscrone nestles quietly amid the dunes in County Sligo

Royal Portrush Golf Club is steeped in history, not just in the golfing sense. It is overlooked by Dunluce Castle. The romantic ruins of this thirteenth-century Norman fort teeters on the edge of an isolated crag, so close to the precipice that in 1693 some of it actually fell into the sea during a storm. Founded in 1888, the club became Royal Portrush in 1893, with King Edward VII as patron. It is famous not only for its magnificent links and superb collection of sculptured holes, but also for the fact that it is the only course in Ireland to have hosted the British Open Championship, in 1951.

Max Faulkner was the winner in an area steeped in the longest traditions of Irish golf and where Fred Daly, Ireland's only winner of the Open title, spent much time honing the skills that made him Open winner, at Hoylake in 1947. Daly presented his medal to the club and it remains a treasured memento in the imposing clubhouse.

Unquestionably, the Killarney Golf and Fishing Club is one of the world's foremost golfing meccas, proof positive being that you dare not turn up in the hope of having a round without first booking a tee time.

Majors champions Nick Faldo and Payne Stewart are prominently among the many loud in its praises. 'This is as lovely a venue as I have ever played . . . the course complements the beautiful setting. I would gladly play here at any time,' enthused Faldo, coincidentally winner each time the Irish Open was staged on the lakeside Killeen course in 1991 and '92.

Killarney's infamous Par 3, 18th on Mahony's Point, one of the most memorable holes in the game, according to Gene Sarazen.

GREAT OCCASIONS IN IRISH GOLF

CENTRAL TO THE CREATION, healthy state and sustained good image of golf in Ireland today is a moving initiative undertaken by the caring members of Portmarnock Golf Club many years ago.

Concerned that Ireland might not keep abreast of golfing developments elsewhere, they dug deep into their own pockets to inaugurate an Irish Open Championship.

Little could those pioneering men have appreciated the extent to which their dreams would be realised because, since the launching of the first Open Championship at the famous links in 1927, Ireland has indeed become one of the foremost nations in the game.

Portmarnock is acknowledged as the spiritual home of the Irish Open, having staged the biggest international golfing event in Ireland most often. It has also been associated with many other famous occasions that have served to highlight why the Irish have a widely regarded reputation as good organisers — and with an appreciative viewing public.

This reputation has been earned through the success of the British Amateur Championship at Portmarnock in 1949, the British Open at Royal Portrush in 1951, the Dunlop Masters in Portmarnock in 1959 and 1965, the Canada Cup at the same venue in 1960, the Curtis Cup at Royal County Down in 1968 and at Killarney in 1996, the Alcan Tournament at Portmarnock in 1970, the European Amateur Cup in Killarney in 1975 and at Portmarnock in 1996, and the Walker Cup at Portmarnock as the high point of the

Golfing Union of Ireland's Centenary Year celebrations in 1991.

The successful staging of these major events, the uniquely Irish atmosphere they created, the standard of our courses and the heroics of our players through the years is reflected in the multitude clamouring to play the game and the ever increasing number of people who want to visit Ireland in order to savour the unique environment.

Members crossing the estuary at Portmarnock in the early years of the century, and the clubhouse today with the winter visitation of brent geese on the foreshore.

It is no wonder that golf in Ireland plays such a key role in the economy by way of tourism, business and employment.

With the exception of the British Open, no event on the European calendar can compare with the Irish Open in terms of its quality entry and standard of courses on which it has been played, especially since it was revived in 1975 and built to its current prominence. The roll-call of winners reads like a golfing who's who.

In keeping with the old adage that tournament winners are two a penny but that Open champions are a breed apart, you get a fair indication of the status of the Irish Open by taking account of Ben Crenshaw, Hubert Green, Seve Ballesteros, Jose Maria Olazabal, Nick Faldo, Ian Woosnam, Colin Montgomerie and Bernhard Langer heading the statistics.

All the while, an appreciative Irish public, weaned on a rich diet of performances by the world's greatest players — Tom Watson, Gary Player, Greg Norman, Curtis Strange, Lee Trevino, Johnnie Miller, Tom Weiskopf, Tom Kite, John Daly and so many more — have built up a warm liaison with these overseas giants.

Yet, much as they have been embraced by the depth of renowned Irish hospitality, there is, all the while, the fervent hope that this most prestigious crown can be kept at home.

Jovial Max MacCready, 1949 British amateur champion in historic circumstances.

Colourful John O'Leary, a member of the élite home-bred Irish Open winners' circle.

Demonstrative Christy O'Connor, Jnr — provided magic golfing moments at Woodbrook in 1975.

Venerable Harry Bradshaw, a double Irish Open winner.

Fred Daly (1946), Harry Bradshaw (1947 and 1949), Christy O'Connor, Jnr (1975) and John O'Leary (1982) stand apart in the earnest quest to repel the foreign invasion.

In being crowned first ever home champion, popular Fred Daly rekindled memories of the part Portmarnock members had played in having the event staged in the first instance. The great Bobby Locke was presented as the star turn at Portmarnock when the Open was first played after a break since 1939 caused by World War II.

The draw and outcome of the first professional golf tournament ever staged in Ireland, organised and hosted by Royal Portrush, in 1895. Decided by match-play, the Professional Golf Tournament was won by the famous Alexander 'Sandy' Herd, who became the club's first professional. He beat Harry Vardon, then a comparatively little known player, who was to win the first of his British Open Championship titles the following year.

Professional tournament golf in Ireland can trace its origins to 1895 to Royal Portrush where the first formal match play competition among professional players was held.

There were many overseas entries, including a foursome, each of whom had won the British Open — Harry Vardon, Willie Fernie, Jack White and Alexander (Sandy) Herd.

The competition was won by Herd, a Scot, later to gain infamy by the manner in which he acquired the 'revolutionary' new Haskell ball from America — it is said he paid eight times over the odds on the black market — to play in the Open Championship of 1902 at Hoylake.

In that Open, Herd beat Vardon and James Braid by a shot, even though legend has it that the latest new Haskell ball, said to give upwards of 30 additional yards off the tee to the good players, was out of shape at the finish, with parts of its wound rubber interior actually visible!

Club-promoted tournaments continued at Portrush till 1900, until replaced in 1907 by the Irish Professional Championship.

In the landmark 1895 event, Herd defeated Harry Vardon, who was then an almost unknown 24-year-old and who, in the following year, was to win the first of his six British Opens, a record preserved to this day.

Sandy Herd.

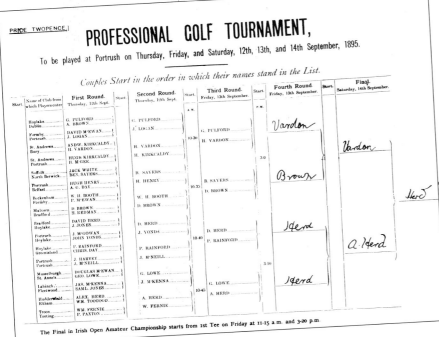

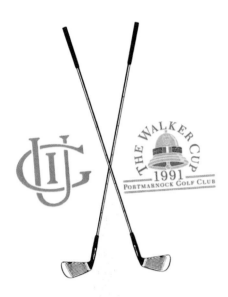

ÉIRE   CLÚDACH CHÉAD LAE   POST

*Commemorative 1991 Walker Cup and GUI
Centenary Year postage stamps.*

*Pensive Padraig Harrington . . . and, far right,
triumphant Paul McGinley, who played in the
historic first-ever staging in Ireland of the
Walker Cup match.*

It was a fitting salute to the Golfing Union of Ireland that the centre piece of their Centenary was the staging of the Walker Cup match, for the first time in Ireland.

September 5th and 6th, 1991 will forever stand as a high point, not alone in Irish golf, but also in the history of the Walker Cup series insofar as the 33rd staging of the great event between the best amateur golfers of Britain and Ireland and the U.S.A. had historic connotations and was seen to be an unqualified success.

That Portmarnock was chosen as venue on the first occasion that the match had been hosted outside mainland Britain when the R and A had choice of venue, was absolutely complimentary. A sell-out attendance of 12,000 made for another landmark.

Garth McGimpsey, Padraig Harrington and Paul McGinley were the Irish players chosen to play and, in weather conditions that varied from heatwave to decided chill beneath leaden skies, it was only the irrepressible skills of Phil Mickelson that eventually turned the absorbing match in America's favour, by the margin of 14-10.

A domestic feature for the record, all ticket attendance, was a fabulous wedge shot, from 110 yards range, to the 18th green, hit by Paul McGinley that set up victory, in partnership with Liam White, over Mickelson and Bob May.

Furthermore, McGimpsey added handsomely to his reputation as one of Britain and Ireland's greatest ever amateur players by beating the formidable Mike Sposa on the 18th green.

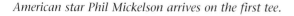
American star Phil Mickelson arrives on the first tee.

Paul McGinley.

*Extrovert Max
Faulkner, winner of the
only British Open
Championship staged
in Ireland, at Royal
Portrush, 1951.*

*Rhythmic Christy
O'Connor, Snr, in
classic finishing pose.
He made his British
Open debut at Royal
Portrush in 1951.*

Max Faulkner won the only British Open Championship staged in Ireland, at Royal Portrush in 1951.

A flamboyant character, usually attired in plus-fours, it is said that the Englishman actually signed his autograph, 'Max Faulkner, Open champion', before going out to play in the last round!

Faulkner scored 71-70-70-74, the critical element being identified as his second round when he was safely back in the clubhouse protected from the wind and rain that was to prove the undoing of his challengers.

Although he had some anxious moments in the final round, Faulkner won by 2 shots from the Argentinian, Antonio Cerda, whose last hope disappeared when he ran up a 6 at the infamous par three 14th, known universally as Calamity!

Although there were 180 entries, of which 85 professionals and 13 amateurs qualified, the historic occasion was played against a backdrop of disgruntlement when the amateur Frank Stranahan was the only one of an anticipated big American contingent to show up. Men like Jimmy Demaret, Johnny Bulla and Skee Rigel were expected to add some impetus to an event struggling to command international status.

The South African, Bobby Locke, was hot favourite to win his third British Open title in a row and a memory preserved by Christy O'Connor, Snr, who was playing in his first ever Open Championship, is of a bookmaker, who had somehow illicitly set up stall, crying out odds of 5/2 Bobby Locke as he was being bundled not once, but twice, off the course!

In any event, Locke's challenge in a high-scoring championship was a timid one as he finished 8 shots behind.

The Portrush British Open was also noted for the debut made by one P. W. Thomson (Australia), the Melbourne Tiger as he was to become known, finishing in a tie for sixth place. That first taste of links golf for Peter Thomson, then a 21-year-old on his first explorative golf trip outside Australia, was of course the precursor to gaining later fame as a five-times winner.

There were high hopes that Fred Daly, on his home course, and Harry Bradshaw, winner of the Irish Open over the same Dunluce links a few years previously, might mark the occasion by having an Irishman crowned champion. It was not to be, however, as Daly, a winner of the championship, in 1947, scored 74-70-75-73 for fourth place and Bradshaw, his chances damaged by an opening round of 80, finished 13th with rallying rounds of 71-74-71.

Christy O'Connor, his expenses paid by supportive Tuam club members where he had taken up his first formal attachment as a club professional, finished in 19th place. Like Bradshaw, he also started with a millstone when taking 79 in his first round.

A frequent talking point among golfers is the prospect of a return to Ireland of the Open Championship. The Royal and Ancient is quite disposed to the notion and the St Andrews authorities have pointed out that it can be played anywhere within its jurisdiction as the governing body of amateur golf, outside America.

General secretary, Michael Bonallack, is on record as saying: 'The Republic of Ireland is certainly qualified and on a personal note I would see Portmarnock as an ideal venue.'

The political climate down through the years has militated against the cause, although Royal Portrush, with a fine tradition of hosting major events, and Royal County Down, in the foothills of the Mountains of Mourne, must still cherish the hope.

Great Irish venues: Mount Juliet and Killarney.

When George Duncan won the inaugural Irish Open at Portmarnock in 1927, there unfolded one of the most remarkable stories ever told in the game.

Going into the final round, the 34-year-old club professional from Wentworth found himself 14 shots behind his own assistant Jack Smith. As the rain belted down and wind also caused havoc with the scoring, the wily Duncan lined his body with brown paper to protect himself against the vile elements.

The upshot was that he produced an incredible 74 despite the conditions, and with Smith taking 91, Duncan made up the vast scoring difference to win the title.

Described by James Braid as 'the most extraordinary golfer I have ever seen', Duncan's place in golfing history is also assured by the manner of his quite remarkable victory in the British Open of 1920.

After two rounds at Deal he trailed Abe Mitchell by 13 strokes, but a third round of 71 with a new driver worked wonders. He shot a morning round of 71 against 84 by Mitchell, followed by 72 in the afternoon against 76 by the faltering runaway halfway leader. To this day, Duncan's effort of winning from a position of 13 shots behind after 36 holes and level after 54 remains as a British Open Championship record.

The players seemed to be unhappy, however, that there was no increase in the prize money, so some Portmarnock members, as their predecessors had done before them, got together and put up £200 as an inducement to the player who could break 70.

It was a sufficient enticement to bring the best out of Daly when a third round 69 backboned a 4 stroke winning effort from Locke, who had been the favourite to win.

The following year at Portrush, Harry Bradshaw won the first of his two Irish Opens against a field of 67 — with prize money of £1,500 — and, amid even more emotional scenes two years later at Belvoir Park, Bradshaw won again.

Set against the cruel background of how he had lost to Bobby Locke in the British Open a short while earlier, the fans turned out in their thousands to the rolling parkland course that commands such a tranquil setting in the southern suburbs of Belfast.

The avuncular Brad, with an ever ready smile and handshake, reciprocated that goodwill as he shot rounds of 70-71-72-73 to reverse the tragic British Open result. With just one shot in it at the climax, the tense drama of the occasion endured to the very end as Locke's defiant effort to force a play-off saw his determined putt stop an inch from the hole!

When the biting economic climate of the 1950s caused the Irish Open to be discontinued, it was fully twenty-two years before a relaunch took place. Naturally there was delight throughout the Irish sporting fraternity which heralded the move, the true wisdom of which is now fully manifest.

The decision to try and emulate the heady first days of the Irish Open was based on the success of the many tournaments promoted by the P. J. Carroll company since the early 1960s and which had gained unprecedented appeal on the strength of Christy O'Connor's domination of the event.

Central to the growth in popularity and the spread of golf throughout Ireland had been the staging of major tournaments that were to capture the popular imagination. The British Open at Royal Portrush in 1951, representing the only time that it has been played outside mainland Britain, played its part, as indeed did the decision to allocate to Portmarnock in 1949 the British Amateur Championship which was won by Max McCready.

The acclaim accorded to Joe Carr, Harry Bradshaw and Christy O'Connor, as they impacted on amateur and professional golf in Britain from this point onwards, further helped to enhance the reputation of Ireland as a golfing nation.

As Carr established himself as the leading amateur of Europe, and Bradshaw and O'Connor became established on the British circuit as regular tournament winners and the backbone of successive Ryder Cup teams, it is generally held that events of the late 1950s and early 1960s provided the benchmark from which the game of golf in Ireland today traces its spectacular growth.

The staging at Portmarnock of the Dunlop Masters tournament, very much a prestige event of the time, in 1959 and 1965 (though the latter was marred early on by vile weather), played a huge part. But it was the occasion of the Canada Cup at Portmarnock in 1960 that truly captured the imagination.

Interest in golf had been escalating when Harry Bradshaw and Christy O'Connor won

the Canada Cup in Mexico City in 1958. So when the initiative followed to bring this multi-nation event to Ireland, the face and image of Irish golf was to be changed forever.

At that time there were barely 200 clubs in Ireland, largely the preserve of a privileged élite partaking in a minority sport. But the victory of Bradshaw and O'Connor in Mexico raised popular curiosity, and the further appeal of the international field assembled in a mid-June heat wave made for an incredibly successful event.

Thousands flocked in shirt sleeves and summer skirts to the sun-drenched and scenic north County Dublin landmark, their anticipation fuelled by the prospect of cheering on the Irish duo of O'Connor

Joe Carr, one of Ireland's greatest golfers, who established himself as the leading amateur in Europe.

Arnold Palmer, whose heroic, dare-devil manner of play won him the hearts of all golfers. He helped inspire a rush to play the game in Ireland.

and Norman Drew, although there was widespread disappointment that Harry Bradshaw had been controversially omitted.

It was estimated that 60,000 spectators swarmed the course and in a magnificently organised event that truly established Portmarnock and Ireland on the modern golfing map of the world, there was some vintage golf, though only glimpses from the Irish representatives who finished fourth, 10 shots behind.

Canada Cup winners, Sam Snead, left, and Arnold Palmer.

The tenacious Gary Player established a course record of 65; graceful Sam Snead and the emerging Arnold Palmer won the team event for the United States; and Belgium's Flory van Donck won the individual title.

There was much admiration for the stylishly elegant figure of van Donck. The Irish public also paid homage to Player, the reigning British Open champion, and there was unbounded admiration for the enduring skills of Snead, 48 years of age and with his classically fluent swing still intact.

Yet it was Arnold Palmer who won the hearts of the crowd. The man who is credited with having revolutionised the image of the game in America in this great period of golfing change was making his first ever tournament appearance outside the United States and had, at 30 years of age, arrived with a reputation as golf's new People's Champion.

After all, in the spring of that year he had finished with two straight birdies to snatch audaciously his second Masters in three years from the grasp of an expectant Ken Venturi, and in the week prior to his arrival in Ireland, Palmer's daring capacity for finishing strongly is remembered to this day by the

Crowds flocked to watch golf in Ireland during the 1960s when the game gained in popularity by the staging of many big events in the Dublin area.

manner in which he won his only US Open title.

After 54 holes on the Cherry Hills course in Colorado, Palmer's supporters had little to cheer as their champion was 7 strokes behind the leader, Mike Souchak. Yet, in a dramatic manner that characterised so much of his play, Arnie's unmatched flair had contrived to negotiate the treacherous front nine in a facile 30 strokes, with six birdies in 7 holes, to win with a breathless last round of 65.

At Portmarnock also, the heroic, dare-devil manner in which he played as he opened and closed his rounds with a 69, coupled with his friendly disposition towards his new legion of enthralled followers, set him apart. Taking account ultimately of what Palmer was to achieve, there can always be a sense of pride that Ireland had a hand in the making of a golfing god.

'It's the first time I've played a links course and I've learned a lot of shots that will forever stand to me,' the gracious Palmer acknowledged of his Irish experience.

Immediately on departing Portmarnock (and, remember, with the Masters and US Open titles under his belt), he was runner-up to a lucky Kel Nagle at St Andrews after the heartbreak of taking 3 to get down from just short of the 17th in the third round, and 3 from out of the Valley of Sin at the 18th.

In the following two years, however, nothing could stop the rampant Palmer, and his victories at Royal Birkdale and Troon

endure as testament to some of the best golf ever witnessed in British Open history. Enduring, too, is Palmer's publicly quoted belief that his experience at Portmarnock provided the basis of those achievements!

Suddenly, there was unprecedented popular demand for golf in Ireland, fuelled

Nick Faldo's love affair with Irish golf stretches beyond the pursuit of his Irish Open titles.

not only by the local exploits of Irish players but also by the advent of television throughout the country. Great performances in the United States and elsewhere by Arnold Palmer, Jack Nicklaus and others could now be viewed for the first time on television.

Irish golf had at last been taken from a social élite and given to the masses. The face of golf in Ireland was to be changed for ever — and for the better!

One thing complemented the other as the game grew in popularity, not least the consolidation of Ireland as a regular stop-off on the burgeoning professional golf circuit.

The promotion by the P. J. Carroll tobacco company of an annual event, on nine occasions between 1964 and 1974, at the hospitable Woodbrook Club south of Dublin, ensured that the enthusiastic Irish public was being provided with the opportunity to watch the top international players who had become household names as golf flourished world-wide with a commercial explosion.

Winning smile from the maestro.

An older generation will remember with nostalgia how Sunday lunch was regularly abandoned as entire families made their way to the lovely Woodbrook course perched on a clifftop overlooking the Irish Sea to cheer on Christy O'Connor.

Familiar winning partnership throughout the 1960s and 1970s — People's Champion Christy O'Connor, Snr, and his loyal caddie Frank Day.

'Back on the left make way for my man,' echoed the plaintive cries of loyal caddie Frank Day as corridors were created through the crowds so that Christy could proceed.

And of course the great man thrived, as he readily acknowledged the part Ireland's growing legion of golf lovers played in his career.

The crowds were worth shots to me. There was nothing I relished more than a gallery. The roar of the crowd was music in my ears and I thrived on the tournament opportunity of getting the British and other overseas pros to Ireland and into my own backyard.

I recall the halcyon days from 1960 to 1972 when I won either the Irish Hospitals' Tournament at Woodbrook, the Gallaher Ulster Open at Shandon Park in Belfast or the Carroll's tournaments at Woodbrook and Royal Dublin on as many as nine occasions.

I have no doubt the partisan Irish crowds were worth bonus shots to me in the psychological sense, as indeed other players would benefit in their home ground. A perk of the trade is that if, as I luckily did, have a battalion of spectators with me, there was not much fear of losing a ball in the rough with anything up to 10,000 pairs of eyes joining in the search.

But I never took illegal advantage of my supporters. There is a saying among the pros, 'Don't be shy, there's a crowd at the back,' meaning that you can afford to hit an attacking shot and the sheer masses of bodies will prevent the ball from running through the green.

Five times at Woodbrook, O'Connor rewarded his many admirers by winning major events, though it was an occasion at his beloved Royal Dublin that he might cherish most.

Philip Walton, left and Ian Woosnam, locked in a famous Irish Open battle.

It was in 1966 that he gave the profile of the game in Ireland another massive boost by the manner of his victory. With three holes left to play, O'Connor appeared to be in a hopeless position as his old adversary, the Scot, Eric Brown, was safely in the clubhouse, having birdied two of the last three holes to post a 69 for a total of 274. The first prize was £1,000 and, really, Brown had a right to put it in his pocket because at that stage O'Connor was on the 16th tee and required a birdie at each of the last three holes to force a tie. In vintage O'Connor fashion, however, and to cheers of delight that to this day echo above the Dollymount club, O'Connor unleashed a demonstration of virtuoso golf.

A three wood tee shot to within 20 feet of the pin at the 251 yard 16th turned improbability into hope, as down went the putt for an eagle to the gasps of the massed crowds. Enthusiasm threatened to get out of hand when the local hero then sank another 20 footer on the 17th green, a birdie that put O'Connor in a tie for the lead.

Determined Colin Montgomerie traverses the water surrounding the island Par 3, 17th green en route to dramatic victory in the Irish Open at Druid's Glen.

Legendary South African Bobby Locke, five times British Open champion, playing from the 4th tee at Portstewart during the qualifying rounds for the 1951 British Open Championship staged at near-by Royal Portrush.

The beauty of Mount Juliet on and off the Jack Nicklaus designed course —
scene of many great moments in Irish golf.

iron across the infamous out-of-bounds 'garden' that fronts the green when the short cut across the left-to-right dog leg is taken.

And, sure enough, O'Connor also executed that shot with uncanny accuracy, the ball floating precisely on its intended flight path, grazing the flagstick as it landed, finishing just 10 feet from the hole.

When his putt went down for an eagle, there were scenes of enthusiasm rarely witnessed since at any Irish sporting event. Christy O'Connor had incredibly won a tournament that had seemed out of the question 45 minutes earlier. Eagle, birdie, eagle (2-3-3) was the astonishing finish.

It now seemed inevitable that the Carroll's tournaments should be upgraded, and when Pat Heneghan, the man behind the great Carroll's success story, had the foresight to revive the Irish Open Championship, the game in Ireland was to take off on yet another spiral of growth.

It seemed appropriate also that the first Irish Open to be played since 1953 should be hosted by Woodbrook — and, indeed, that the event should remain synonymous with the name O'Connor. On this occasion, however, it was Christy O'Connor, Jnr, nephew of the great man, who scaled the heights, rebuffing an international field that included the recently crowned British Open

Now he needed one more birdie at the 18th to snatch victory out of Brown's pocket.

He chose his trusty spoon off the tee and when the hard-pressed stewards got the thousands of excited fans into some semblance of order, their man landed the drive more or less where he had visualised. The ball came to rest hard to the right-hand side of the fairway, close by the out-of-bounds ditch. From that strategically precise spot it was a three

champion Tom Watson, with a 21 under par winning performance. Not to be totally eclipsed, uncle Christy shared some of the glory, holing in one at the 17th to win the champagne with which he greeted his nephew in celebration.

When the decision was taken to return the Irish Open to its spiritual home at Portmarnock, there was a brief period of American circuit player dominance as Ben Crenshaw in 1976 and Hubert Green the following year won the championship.

However, what might have been an American stranglehold was to be quickly ended and remained rebuffed for many years as a shift in the balance of world golfing power moved to Europe, with the emergence of a new generation of players such as Seve Ballesteros, Sam Torrance, Bernhard Langer, Ian Woosnam, Jose Maria Olazabal, Nick Faldo and Colin Montgomerie, all of whom served a critical part of their apprenticeship at the Irish Open.

FRED DALY

Big crowds flocked to Killarney to watch international star line-ups in memorable Irish Open Championships.

QUOTATIONS ABOUT IRISH GOLF

Ireland was always popular as a golfing destination, to judge by the sentiments expressed by some of the great and legendary players who travelled across the Irish Sea in search of competition around the turn of the century.

Recalling that period, J. H. Taylor wrote very favourably about golf and Ireland. For example, in 1902, in an effusive proclamation, he expressed the opinion:

Golf may eventually prove to be the salvation of the country at large. The game will bring money from all quarters. Trade will naturally follow its wake, for tourists will cross the Irish Sea — not for the mountains, the lakes or the fishing, but for the golf.

This is not a fancy picture. There are already signs of the attractions of the game in Ireland and I have no doubt that time will prove the correctness of my estimate.

Ireland's golfing capabilities have just been tapped and I have little hesitation stating that before many years have passed it will have steadily risen into the position of a great golfing country. Its advantages are many.

There you can find without great difficulty a large number of very natural courses, magnificent in their quality and the extent of virgin ground yet to be opened up by the golf pioneer is an almost unthinkable quantity.

Irish turf is like velvet in its texture and the very finest putting greens in the world are to be found there. This is only what one might expect from the great climatic influences that are at work all the year round. Much more rain falls in Ireland than in England, the whole atmosphere is genial and moist in character and so the turf is springy, soft and as true as could be desired by the most fastidious of golfers.

Vardon was another of the game's pioneering legends to portray Ireland in the best light — and with a delightful touch of humour.

An experience he had during one of the early events at Portrush concerns the caustic Scot, Andrew Kirkaldy, one of three golfing brothers and by all accounts one of the best players from the St Andrews district never to win the British Open.

Vardon recalls that he had been drawn to play Kirkaldy and when introduced to him, the blunt and abrupt greeting he got was: 'Youngster, what the hell do you want to come all this way to Portrush for? You've no earthly chance against me.'

Vardon recalled: 'The following day a heavy wind was blowing and at the first hole I had a putt of not more than a yard to secure the lead. Every moment the ball threatened to roll over and I waited for it to steady itself. The waiting appeared to get on Andrew's nerves and he soon exclaimed: "Man, d'ye ken I'm caul . . . are ye gaun to keep me waiting here a nicht!"' And Vardon duly went on to win.

LADIES' GOLF IN IRELAND

T HE STORY OF LADIES' GOLF IN IRELAND bears a close resemblance to that of the men. It too was inspired by a strong Scottish influence and nurtured by determined passion.

By coincidence, both codes hold the proud honour of having established the first national unions. The Golfing Union of Ireland was formed in 1891 and the Irish Ladies' Golf Union was established two years later.

In each instance, the preliminary steps had Scottish antecedents. In the case of the ladies, the initiative was taken by the wife of a Group Captain Wright of the Scottish Light Infantry. Her presence on the fairways of Ireland's oldest established club, Royal Belfast, at Holywood, County Down, was causing considerable curiosity.

It was about 1887 — the Belfast Club having been founded in 1881, assuming the Royal prefix four years later — and if the sight of a lady golfer was indeed a rare one, it aroused sufficient interest to inspire others.

Mrs Wright presented a set of clubs to her friend, Miss C. E. McGee, who became so enthusiastic about the game that she soon persuaded others to follow suit. One year later, in 1887, the Holywood Ladies' Golf Club was formed by seven enthusiasts!

Taking account of the inherent prejudices of the day, it took a determined group of women to pursue their cause.

Group of ladies assembled for play in 1893 when history records the proposal that: 'a Union of the Irish Ladies' Golf Clubs be and is hereby formed and shall be called The Irish Ladies' Golf Union'.

Such was their enthusiasm, however, that following the lead of the Holywood ladies, other clubs, notably Killymoon, Newcastle, Portrush, Dungannon and Belmont came into existence, as the ladies persuaded their menfolk to extend to them the same goodwill as exemplified by the Royal Belfast Club.

Thus, with the ladies' movement gathering momentum, it was not long until the far-sighted Miss McGee led another campaign, this time to further broaden the appeal of women's golf by giving it a national identity.

Women at play in 1900 accompanied by their caddies!

So the pages of history record that on Friday, 15 December 1893, at a meeting of sixteen people representing Royal Belfast, Dungannon and Royal County Golf Club, Portrush, it was agreed, as proposed by Miss Cox, and seconded by the redoubtable Miss McGee: 'In the interests of golf in Ireland, it is desirable that a Union of the Irish Ladies' Golf Clubs be and is hereby formed and shall be called The Irish Ladies' Golf Union.'

A proposal: 'That an annual Championship meeting be held and that the first be at Carnalea in April 1894, at Portrush in 1895 and at Newcastle in 1896', was also important as nothing underscores more the thrust of women's golf in Ireland than the successful staging — and winning by Irish players — of major events.

Consider, for example, how Irish players were to make their mark in the premier British Open Championship. It was for the most part an event of curiosity when it was played at Portrush in 1895. Yet, when it returned in 1899 and in the immediate years thereafter, it was dominated by a group of players whose display of talent was an uncanny demonstration of the ease with which Irish women could so quickly take to a game that had been jealously guarded as the preserve of the Irish male.

The trail-blazing influence was best outlined by the remarkable Hezlet sisters, May, Violet and Frances, and their friend, Miss Rhona Adair, who were only in their early teens when the Ladies' Open was held at Portrush in 1895. Yet only four years later they began an extraordinary decade of achievement between them.

The period that can be aptly described as the golden era of Irish ladies' golf can easily be summarised as follows:

1899   Miss M. Hezlet beat Miss Magill by 2 and 1 in final at Newcastle (both ladies were Irish)

1900   Miss Adair wins at Westward Ho

1901   Miss Adair a finalist at Aberdovey

1902   Miss M. Hezlet wins at Deal

1903   Miss Adair beat Miss Walker-Leigh in final at Portrush

1904   Miss M. Hezlet loses final at Troon

1905 Miss M. E. Stuart (Ireland) loses in final at Cromer

1907 Miss M. Hezlet wins final against Miss F. Hezlet at Newcastle

1911 Miss V. Hezlet loses final at Portrush.

Within the week of becoming 17, May Hezlet won the Irish and British titles in 1899, defeating her friend Rhona Adair in the British final; but in 1900 Miss Adair duplicated May Hezlet's double, beating another of the Hezlet sisters, Violet, in the Irish Championship. May, Violet and Frances contested nine of the twelve Irish Championships between 1898 and 1909, and on each occasion there was at least one of them in the final.

All the while, Miss Adair was also to the forefront of affairs, winning the Irish title four years in a row from 1900 and winning the British Open again in 1903. She also travelled to the United States and captured the

imagination of many Americans by the length she could hit the ball and also by the manner in which she won sixteen of the seventeen events she played in while on a tour in 1903. On one occasion during her American trip she astounded onlookers by carrying a shot fully 170 yards across a lake.

Yet, for all this trail blazing, a source of disappointment within the women's golf movement was the seeming reluctance of clubs from the South of Ireland to become affiliated to the Union. Only Foxrock, which

became the first in 1897, bringing the strength of the Union to 13 clubs, followed by Cork in 1901, Greenore the following year, and then Lahinch in 1904, were in the fold.

At this point, two decisions taken were to greatly enhance the spread of the game and the strength of the Irish Ladies' Golf Union.

First was the proposal, 'with a view to furthering the sphere of golf and to arouse the interest of Southern players' that the Irish Championship be staged in Lahinch in 1904

The distinctive style of ladies playing golf in 1894.

Miss Clara Mulligan, Irish lady champion in 1894 and elected first Honorary Secretary of the ILGU.

and, second, that a Union annual meeting be held in Dublin. The meeting duly took place in 1906 at the old Metropole Hotel in Sackville Street (now called O'Connell Street).

In a letter of appeal to all lady golfers of the time, the Union honorary secretary, Miss C. L. Neil, wrote: 'The Union was first started in Belfast ten years ago and the first rule runs thus: "Any ladies' golf club in Ireland, having a designation and golfing green, shall be admissible into the Golf Union. There are now eighteen clubs in the Union, the only ones outside Ulster being Greenore, Foxrock and Cork. This year's Championship is to be held at Lahinch where we hope for a large entry from clubs that have not yet joined the Union."'

Her marketing ploy worked as there was an enthusiastic response. Utilising the West Clare Railway line, which was to become immortalised in song by Percy French, and staying in the splendour of the old Golf Links Hotel, where reports of the era tell of 'the golfers partaking of hot and cold sea water baths during their sojourn', the wisdom of the decision was soon to manifest itself.

A rapid growth in Union affiliations quickly followed as the cause was helped by the victory at Lahinch of May Hezlet in a successful championship, although she defeated the host club's first designated Lady Captain, Miss Florence Walker-Leigh.

Lahinch had been the nineteenth club to join the Union in 1904, but within six years fifteen more clubs from beyond Ulster had taken up ILGU status. Greystones, Carrickmines, Killiney and Sutton joined in 1905–06; The Island, Malahide, Bray and County Sligo joined a year later, and by 1910, Rathfarnham, Killarney, Tramore, Tralee,

Set against Ireland's long and distinguished contribution to the Curtis Cup, it was disappointing that on the two occasions that the match against the USA was staged in Ireland, there was no Irish player on the British and Irish team! At Royal County Down, Newcastle, in 1968, the reigning Irish champion, Elaine Bradshaw, was controversially omitted. And when the match was played in the Republic of Ireland for the first time, at Killarney in 1996, again no Irish player found favour.

Coincidentally, on both occasions Ireland provided the home team's non-playing captain. At Royal County Down, Mrs Zara Bolton who resided in Portrush took charge as Britain and Ireland lost by $10\frac{1}{2}$–$7\frac{1}{2}$ and at Killarney, when 10,000 spectators thronged the course running alongside the famous lakes, Mrs Ita Butler had the distinction of inspiring the home team to an $11\frac{1}{2}$–$6\frac{1}{2}$ win.

Mrs Butler (née Burke) had played in the corresponding match in 1966 in Hot Springs, Virginia, winning two of her three games.

Killarney, 1996: A memorable moment in Irish golf — Ita Butler, captain of the winning British and Irish team, celebrates with team members at the conclusion of the first Curtis Cup match to be staged in the Republic of Ireland.

Limerick, Hermitage and Milltown had also joined the Union.

The ladies' game throughout Ireland was thriving and not even World War I could shake its foundations.

A decision was taken at the annual meeting in December 1918 'to resume all ILGU business' and by 1920 there were 63 affiliated clubs. By 1935 the figure had risen to 165, leading to the appointment of the Union's first full-time executive in 1946.

May Hezlet — a major influence in the development of ladies' golf in Ireland.

DUBLIN
Hotel Metropole,
SACKVILLE STREET
(Next to the General Post Office).

Train and Tram Centre for all the Suburban Golf Links.

One Hundred Bedrooms.　　　Most Modern Arrangements.
PASSENGER LIFT TO ALL FLOORS.
Excellent Cuisine, - - Moderate Charges.

Restaurant Department Open to Resident Visitors.

Tariff and Descriptive Particulars on Application to the MANAGER.
Telegrams : 'METROPOLE, DUBLIN..'　　Telephones : Hotel, 422 ; Restaurant, 3033.

The old Hotel Metropole on Dublin's Sackville Street (now O'Connell Street), where a critical meeting of the Union was held in 1906 'with a view to furthering the sphere of golf and to arouse the interest of Southern players'.

THIS IS THE BALL
to win competitions,
"THE BLUE DOT HEAVY MERSEY."
Send 2/- P.O. mentioning the name of your Club and test one.
To be had from all Professionals and Leading Athletic Stores.

THE HELSBY Co. (British Insulated and Helsby Cables, Ltd.) HELSBY, near, WARRINGTON.
LONDON—Lennox House, Norfolk Street, Strand.   GLASGOW—177 West George Street.   BIRMINGHAM—19 Barwick Street.
DUBLIN—17 Crow Street (Dame Street).   BELFAST—11 Queen Street.   MANCHESTER—3 Parsonage, Blackfriars.
NEWCASTLE-ON-TYNE—Ward's Buildings, 33 Highbridge.   CARDIFF—1 and 2 Western Mail Chambers.

*Driving on 'Tennis'
hole, ladies' course,
Ballycastle.*

Portsalon golf links, driving ·······························
from the 5th tee.

The post of secretary was given to Miss Violet Hezlet, at an annual salary of £125. It was an inspired appointment because until her retirement in 1975 she discharged her duties with such admirable efficiency that she was unanimously nominated in 1976 by the Irish Golf Writers' Association for their first award for Distinguished Services to Irish Golf.

If the Hezlet sisters and Rhona Adair, to be followed among others by Mabel Harrison and Patsy Jameson, were the pioneers in establishing the status of Ireland by way of their achievements, the consolidation of the game after the World War II period was built upon the outstanding performances of many more players.

Set against the growing appeal of the game in general and especially the attention being won by Ireland's men, both amateur and professional, it was of immense importance and satisfaction to Ireland's women's golfing community that they could count among their number such great players as Clarrie Reddan (née Tiernan), Kitty MacCann, Philomena Garvey, Ita Butler, Elaine Bradshaw, Mary McKenna, Maureen Madill, Claire Robinson, Lillian Behan, Claire Hourihane and Eileen Rose Power (née McDaid).

Proudly consigned among the many imperishable milestones of the first century of ladies' golf in Ireland are the achievements of winning the European Team Championship of 1979 and 1983.

It was a brave undertaking by the ILGU to host the 14 Nations Championship for the first time in Ireland in 1979, and it was equally perceptive to nominate the Hermitage Club, as its lovely setting amid oaks, wych-elms and limes was so complementary to the cosmopolitan nature of the great occasion.

The Irish team comprised Susan Gorman, Claire Nesbitt, Mary McKenna, Maureen Madill, Rhona Hegarty and Mary Gorry, with Maire O'Donnell as non-playing captain, and their achievement of beating West Germany by a clear-cut 6–1 in the final had the added historical significance of Ireland's victory being the first major team championship won since the Home International Championship 72 years before!

Also, there was an appropriate sense of history about their second triumph in 1983, given that the venue was Royal Waterloo, near Brussels.

Waterloo, scene of Napoleon's famous demise in 1815, became the stage of unrestrained celebration among the 16 competing nations, as Mary McKenna and Maureen Madill, the only survivors from Hermitage, along with Claire Hourihane, Eavan Higgins and the sisters, Philomena and Carol Wickham, were led to glory by Ann Heskin as non-playing captain and Gerry Costello as her assistant — the rampant Irish team beating England by a crushing $5\frac{1}{2}$–$1\frac{1}{2}$ margin in the final.

The Baltray pair of Clarrie Reddan (Tiernan) and Philomena Garvey brought particular fame to women's golf.

The war years deprived Clarrie of showing the world just how good a player she really was. She had made her mark in 1936 at Ballybunion, aged only 20, when she was crowned Irish champion. A year later she won the New Jersey Championship; in 1938 she was capped in the Curtis Cup, emerging with an unbeaten record, before going on to reach the final of the Canadian Open where she lost only on the final green.

When sport resumed after the war, it was a measure of Mrs Reddan's golfing facility that she could take up where she had left off six years previously by again reaching the final of the Irish championship at Lahinch in 1946 where, by coincidence, her opponent was her Baltray village neighbour, Philomena Garvey.

Presentation ceremony after the final of the Irish Ladies' Championship, Ballybunion, 1932 with Mr J. Clarke, Captain, Ballybunion, presenting Miss Betty Latchford (right) with the cup. Included, left to right, Mrs Cuthell, President, ILGU, Mrs Smith, Honorary Secretary, ILGU, Mr John Macaulay, Club President and Mr William MacCarthy, Club Honorary Secretary.

Their achievements included Ireland's telling Curtis Cup contribution, the European Team Championship triumphs of 1979 and 1983, further success in the Home International matches and the British Amateur Open titles, match play and medal, collected by Mrs MacCann and then by Misses Garvey, Madill, McKenna, Behan and Hourihane.

THEODORE HAMBLIN
LIMITED
Dispensing Opticians
Makers of Spectacles to
Surgeons' Prescriptions only

HAMBLINS'
"FULL-FIELD" SPECTACLES
for
GOLF

Fitted with
"SALVOC"
SAFETY LENSES
which even if smashed
will not splinter.

THEODORE HAMBLIN LIM
DISPENSING OPTICIANS
15, WIGMORE STREET, LONDO
and at
MANCHESTER, LIVERPOOL, SHEFFIELD, LEEDS, EDINBURGH, N
UPON-TYNE, BOURNEMOUTH, WINDSOR, CHESTERFIELD, KI

Lillywhites
of PICCADILLY CIRCUS
LONDON, W.1

A NEW
GOLF
SUIT
Beige Skirt and
Shirt with Nigger
Jersey Top.
Also in Grey with
Navy Top.

8 Gns.

SPORTS
WEAR

Illustrated Brochure of
Golf and Sports Wear
Post Free on request.

Legendary pairing — Fred Daly and Philomena Garvey. Miss Garvey proudly displays the British Championship trophy after a famous victory at Gleneagles.

That match is considered by Irish sporting historians as one of the outstanding deciders, at the climax of which the emerging Miss Garvey won on the 39th hole with the aid of a stymie (now outlawed, whereby a player's line to the hole could be blocked by an opponent's ball).

This was to be the first of fifteen Irish titles to be won by Philomena Garvey in a remarkable career. In the period 1946 to 1963 she was well nigh unbeatable, winning fourteen out of a possible eighteen titles. The fifteenth followed as a sweet swan-song at Royal Portrush in 1970 when she was reinstated as an amateur, having been a professional from 1964 to 1968.

It is an accurate measure of Philomena Garvey's standing in Irish golf that when she decided to turn professional, the Irish Ladies' Golf Union was sufficiently moved to record in the minutes of the 71st Annual General Meeting: 'Philomena Garvey was made a Life President of the Union in recognition of her magnificent golf record and prestige she has brought to Ireland through the game of golf.'

Philomena Garvey played for Ireland as an amateur from 1946 to 1963. She also took part in six Curtis Cup matches between 1948 and 1960, declining to play in another because she objected to the Union Jack of Britain being used as the official team badge. However, her record in the British Amateur Open Championship was frustrating: five times she reached the final, with only one victory in 1957 at Gleneagles when she beat the great Jessie Valentine of Scotland.

Irish Championship finalists in 1936 — Clarrie Reddan (née Tiernan) and Sybil Moore.

One of the most memorable matches ever staged was contested between two of the game's most remarkable people, the prodigy Rhona Adair of the Royal Portrush Club and the game's patriarchal legend, Old Tom Morris. It was in July 1899 Morris, 77 years of age and Miss Adair, a mere 16-year-old, took part in a challenge match at St Andrews.

By all accounts, and in keeping with that romantic era in golf, the venerable Morris, British Open winner on four occasions, still enjoyed playing 36 hole matches on the same day, although in this instance it is said he vowed, 'I'll no be licked by a lassie', before stepping on to the first tee of the Old Course to tackle the precocious Irish teenager who already had the reputation of being able to hit the ball further than any other woman!

Harold Hilton, early golf's most famous amateur and twice winner of the British Open title, outlined the merits of the young Irish girl when he wrote:

'Lady players, as a rule, appear to persuade the ball on its way; Miss Adair, on the contrary, avoids such constrictions on her methods by hitting very hard indeed. There is a determination and firmness in her address which is most fascinating to watch. She stands up to the ball in a manner quite worthy of the sterner sex.'

It was a tribute to the young Irish woman, and an accomplishment that caused quite a stir at the time, when she took golf's great icon to the 18th green and lost the match by only one hole.

Miss Rhona Adair.

An interesting aside to this famous match was that the Irish player was cheered on by Mrs Kitty MacCann, who had won the same title six years previously, as the first Irishwoman to do so since May Hezlet in 1907. Mrs MacCann bridged the 44 year gap with a 4 and 3 win at Broadstone in Dorset over the more fancied Frances (Bunty) Stephens.

And to further demonstrate the Irish flavour of Miss Garvey's long-overdue conquest Kitty MacCann's husband, Pat, who was a veterinary surgeon, had a part to play. He turned first-aid man at the 25th hole where Miss Garvey twisted an ankle she had broken a few years previously, as she was walking downhill from the tee. The vet MacCann strapped up the ailing limb with a handkerchief and the 31-year-old flaxen haired Irish star defiantly limped on to her famous victory.

Old Tom Morris.

Just as Miss Garvey replaced Mrs Reddan as Ireland's leading player, in turn her crown was to go to the young lady she defeated in the 1970 final. Mary McKenna was a worthy heir apparent.

Gifted as one of the longest drivers of the ball, the Dublin bank official from the Donabate Club in north County Dublin made her initial mark as a runner-up to Elaine Bradshaw in the 1968 Irish Championship final at Lahinch. She won it the following year at Ballybunion and was to launch a Garvey-type stranglehold on the trophy, given that in the following twenty years McKenna was to contest a further ten finals, seven of which she won.

All the while she played for Ireland without a break from 1968 to 1991 and again in 1993, her tremendous influence helping in the European Cup triumphs of 1979 and 1983. Furthermore, she made nine Curtis Cup match appearances from 1970 to 1986,

an all-time record for a British and Irish player, to stand proudly in comparison alongside the respective Ryder Cup and Walker Cup record of ten appearances made by compatriots Christy O'Connor, Snr, and Joe Carr.

Miss McKenna was an enthusiastic amateur and declined to pursue a career as a professional. Instead, this was the route taken by Maureen Madill, who as a girl had learned her golf on the links of Portstewart and who made her mark in the game by achieving the most notable double-feat of winning the British Amateur Stroke Play and Match Play titles in 1979 and 1980 respectively.

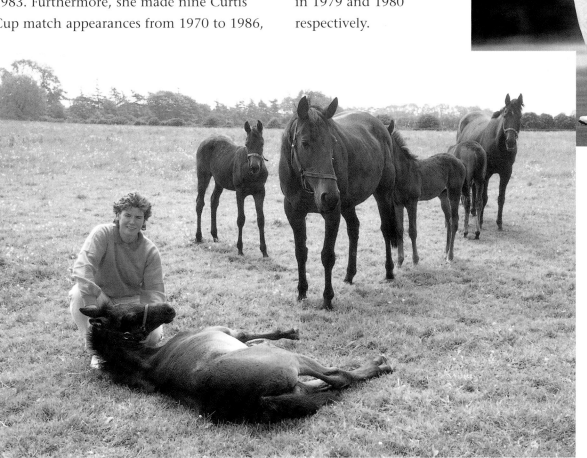

Lillian Behan, winner of the British Championship in 1985, at rest and at play.

THE BOOK OF IRISH GOLF

Two of Ireland's finest lady golfers, Mary McKenna, in multi coloured sweater, and Maureen Madill.

The special honour of achieving a 'British' winner status came to Miss Madill coincidentally in Scotland, as had happened previously to Miss Garvey. Her victory was amid the engaging beauty of Nairn, along the southern shores of the Moray Firth, where the 21-year-old Derry-born woman defeated a noted Australian, Miss Jane Locke, by 2 and 1.

Lillian Behan's surprising victory occured at Ganton in Yorkshire, a distinctive inland venue noted for its links-like texture, when in 1985 she claimed the greatest honour in British and Irish women's golf. She scored a one hole win over Claire Waite from England. The victory by the 20-year-old from the Curragh was as much a surprise in Ireland as it was elsewhere.

Both Madill and Behan turned professional and joined the emerging Women's Professional Tour. After some unrewarding years, Miss Behan returned to the amateur fold. They each made the switch in 1986, Miss Madill having won the British Amateur Open Stroke Play title at Brancept Castle in 1980. It is an honour shared with Mary McKenna, winner at Moseley in 1979, and Claire Hourihane at Blairgowrie in 1986.

A treasured memento belonging to Miss Madill is a letter written to her following the victory by Ireland in the Home Internationals and Triple Crown titles in 1980 at Cruden Bay in Scotland. The note is signed by Violet Hulton, who pointed out that she had been a member of the Irish side that had last won the same title — in 1907. Mrs Hulton was, of course, none other than Violet Hezlet, in whose footsteps it could be said all other Irish women golfers have since followed.

When Lillian Behan followed Maureen Madill as British champion in 1985, the image of Irish ladies' golf in this golden post-war period was proudly kept alight, enriched by Miss Behan, Miss McKenna and Miss Hourihane who all played critical roles at Prairie Dunes, Kansas, in August 1986, when Britain and Ireland won the Curtis Cup. It was the first occasion that a British and Irish team, playing either Curtis, Walker or Ryder Cup competitions, managed to beat the Americans away from home.

A further indication of how Irish players were succeeding internationally was recorded in the Australian and Dutch Open titles won by the Dubliner Maisie Mooney, who was to emigrate to Australia at the height of her career; by the South Atlantic title won by Miss Hourihane in the USA; and also by the most noble effort by Miss McKenna in reaching the semifinal stages of the US Amateur Open in 1980.

While the baton of greatness in the post World War II era had in turn been passed from Clarrie Reddan to Philomena Garvey and on to Mary McKenna, it was the Woodbrook player, Claire Hourihane, who next assumed prominence.

In fact, she was so dominant in the period from 1983 to 1991 that she became Irish champion on five occasions. She lost in two more final appearances but was chosen for four Curtis Cup teams.

Miss Claire Hourihane, five times Irish champion between 1983 and 1991.

Eileen Rose Power, another impressive Irish champion.

A shade different . . . the Par 3, 15th hole in contrasting light on the Glashedy links at Ballyliffen.

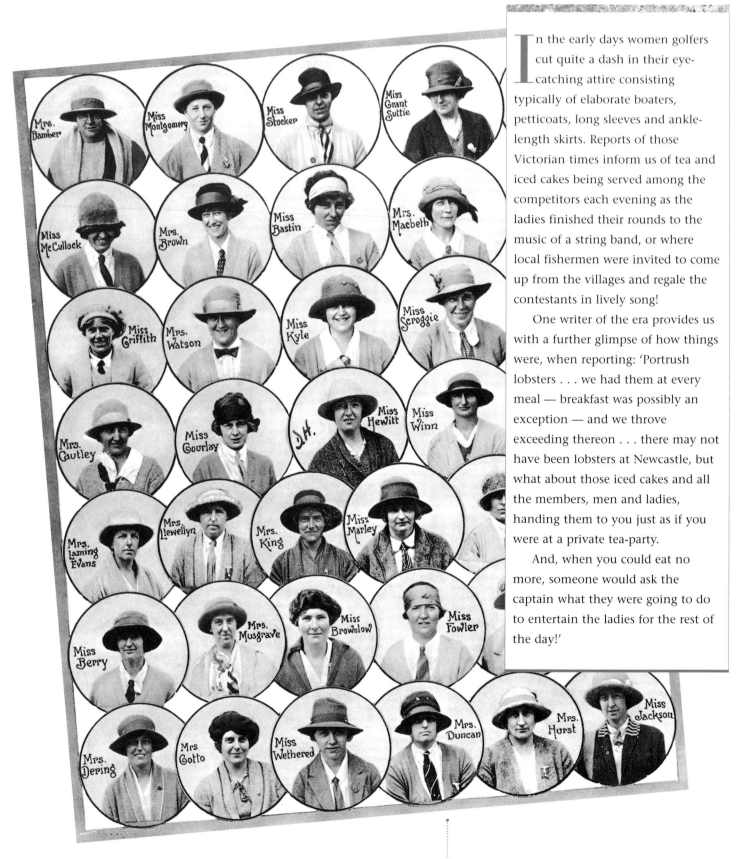

In the early days women golfers cut quite a dash in their eye-catching attire consisting typically of elaborate boaters, petticoats, long sleeves and ankle-length skirts. Reports of those Victorian times inform us of tea and iced cakes being served among the competitors each evening as the ladies finished their rounds to the music of a string band, or where local fishermen were invited to come up from the villages and regale the contestants in lively song!

One writer of the era provides us with a further glimpse of how things were, when reporting: 'Portrush lobsters . . . we had them at every meal — breakfast was possibly an exception — and we throve exceeding thereon . . . there may not have been lobsters at Newcastle, but what about those iced cakes and all the members, men and ladies, handing them to you just as if you were at a private tea-party.

And, when you could eat no more, someone would ask the captain what they were going to do to entertain the ladies for the rest of the day!'

The style of the times — pictorial line up of famous women players assembled for competition.

PLAYERS

I T IS GENERALLY HELD that the question of a golfer's greatness depends ultimately on whether he or she left the game better than when they found it, and on how the game benefited from their involvement. By any standards, the presence of Irish players has contributed handsomely to the game since its formation more than a century ago.

As the popularity of golf began to spread, it was given added momentum by the formation of a handicapping system and by the inauguration of the Irish Amateur Open and the Irish Amateur Close Championships.

A feature of the preliminary practice days was to arrange challenge matches between players from the different countries, opening the way for international competition.

These 'unofficial' matches which began around 1904 led directly to the first official match being staged in 1913 between Ireland and Wales. Ireland continued in regular competition against teams selected by Scotland, the Midlands, Wales and England, until the quadrangular 'Home' International Championship was inaugurated in 1932.

An inevitable result of such competition was the emergence of some consistently good players. One example was Lionel Munn, the acknowledged stylist of the time.

Originally from the North West Club and later from Dublin University and Royal Dublin, Munn was unquestionably the first truly great Irish golfer to make his mark, breaking the monopoly that players from abroad had gained on the Irish Amateur Open Championship by winning a hat-trick of title victories from 1909 to 1911.

In 1911 he further stamped his class by making a clean sweep of the Irish Amateur Championships of the time — the Open, Close and South of Ireland titles.

A reproduction of the actual card returned by Willie Nolan when he scored the first 67 ever recorded at St Andrews in the second qualifying round of the British Open in 1933.

Lionel Munn, the first truly great Irish golfer, who won a hat-trick of Irish Amateur Open Championship titles from 1909 to 1911.

A measure of the tough overseas' opposition — and the recognition given to and the prestige of the Irish Amateur Open — was that the great John Ball, Jnr, Harold Hilton and W. B. Taylor were regular visitors. Between them, this great triumvirate dominated the Irish Amateur Open to such an extent that they took as many as ten titles between 1893 and 1902. But with the foreign invaders finally rebuffed by Munn, Irish players were inspired to emerge from the shadows.

With improving standards of equipment and golf courses, there quickly followed a solid and plentiful supply of players who were also to make their mark on the international scene.

The wonderfully gifted Hezlet sisters and Rhona Adair were setting an example for the ladies. Following Munn, the men also came to the forefront.

There was Michael (Dyke) Moran, a marvellous character from Royal Dublin, who tied for third place in the British Open in 1913 at the age of 25, despite the appalling experience of taking an 89 in the third round.

There was also Willie Nolan, a professional at Portmarnock, so revered in the area that there is a street in neighbouring Baldoyle named after him.

Then there were John Burke, Jimmy Bruen, Cecil Ewing, Harry Bradshaw, Christy O'Connor, Fred Daly, Joe Carr and Philomena Garvey. Some years later came Norman Drew, David Madeley, David Sheahan, Tom Craddock, Garth McGimpsey and also Mary McKenna and Claire Hourihane.

A salute to the memory of the late and legendary Jimmy Bruen, one of Ireland's greatest ever golfers.

Mary McKenna, followed in the footsteps of Philomena Garvey as one of Ireland's best lady players.

The contribution of professionals has been exemplified by the achievements of Eamonn Darcy, Christy O'Connor, Jnr, and Philip Walton, who played such significant roles in winning Ryder Cup matches for Europe. The Irish flag has also been hoisted to mark equally heroic feats by Des Smyth, Ronan Rafferty, John O'Leary and David Feherty, with the baton now passed on to Paul McGinley, Raymond Burns, Darren Clarke and Padraig Harrington.

While those of the knickerbocker, side-whisker and hickory-shafted era set the early standards, inspiration for the beginning of modern times was provided by the legendary Jimmy Bruen. He was, in the opinion of many, the greatest Irish golfer ever.

Born in Belfast in 1920 Bruen became synonymous with Little Island and Muskerry Golf Clubs in Cork, where he spent most of his life. He came to prominence when he took time off from the Presentation Brothers school in 1936 to win the British Boys' Championship at Royal Birkdale, at the age of just 16 years and 3 months. His phenomenal achievement, beating Willie Innes of Scotland by 11 and 9 in the thirty-six hole final, marked the beginning of an unbelievably successful career that was tragically cut short at the age of 26. His right wrist and hand suddenly stopped functioning while he was practising. He was never to recover complete power.

In terms of age comparisons, the only player to match Bruen was Ronan Rafferty who was born in 1964 and who won the Irish Close Championship and tied for the English Amateur Open Stroke Play title at 16 years of age. He made his Irish Amateur team senior debut in the same year, and at 17 years of age played in the Walker Cup.

A group of Irish professionals setting off to play in the post-war 'Victory Tournament' at St Andrews in 1945: (from left) Eddie Hackett, Jack O'Neill, James Cassidy, Norman Wilson, Willie Holly, Kevin O'Connor, John McKenna, Harry Bradshaw, Adam Whiston and Pat O'Connor.

Ireland's young lions: top of the heap, Darren Clarke, taking time out to visit the Giant's Causeway near his home in Portrush and at work accompanied by Seve Ballesteros.

Paul McGinley playing to the 18th green at Royal Lytham and St Anne's where he led for a time in the 1996 British Open.

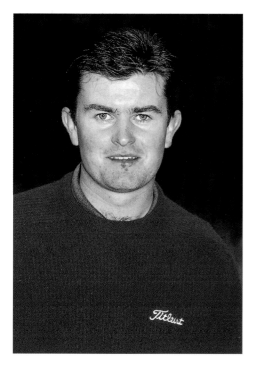

Up and coming Raymond Burns, another star in the making.

McGinley's card, a record 62, en route to victory in Austria.

Far from living in the shadows of past champions, Ireland's young golfing lions are reaching out to set new standards of their own.

Where once it was the old triumvirate of Daly, Bradshaw and O'Connor, Snr, nowadays the Irish assault has been extended to the European Tour and beyond, including the Majors in the USA.

On tour, the Irish stand apart for their collective friendliness and camaraderie.

Hardly a week goes by without one of the present generation of talented players making a bold statement to ensure that Ireland's reputation is kept intact. A measure of their determination is exemplified by the British Open.

It remains a disappointment that Fred Daly's triumph at Hoylake in 1947 represents Ireland's only outright win. While the deeds of Bradshaw and O'Connor are frequently acknowledged, it is important to remember the bold if unavailing attempts of the present generation.

Random highlights are — a sixth place finish by Christy O'Connor, Jnr, to Johnny Miller at Birkdale in 1976; fourth place by Des Smyth, beaten just two shots by Tom Watson at Troon in 1982; third place by O'Connor, Jnr, on that memorable occasion in 1985 when he smashed Henry Cotton's course record 65 at Royal St George's, Sandwich, with ten birdies en route to a 64, only to lose eventually by

two shots to Sandy Lyle; sixth and fourth place by David Feherty at Troon and Turnberry in 1989 and 1994, respectively and, sandwiched in between, was a 68-66-70 finish by Eamonn Darcy at Birkdale in 1991 which gave him fifth place behind Ian Baker-Finch.

Style of Open Champion — Fred Daly.

The stories of Jimmy Bruen's golfing feats are legion. The incredible length he commanded with woods and irons was legendary. He was a superb natural player, with marvellous flair, and the fact that he had a most peculiar loop at the top of his swing merely tended to make him more of a spectacle for awe-struck onlookers. He was at his peak between the ages of 17 and 19 when many regarded him as the best player — amateur or professional — in the world.

Wherever he went he drew gasps of astonishment by his ability to hit the ball vast distances. It was the loop at the top of his over-extended swing (like John Daly among today's long hitters) that enabled him to generate the awesome clubhead speed that propelled the ball so far.

Harry Bradshaw recounted that he played with Bruen on a regular basis over Portmarnock and witnessed him drive the 1st (394 yards), the 2nd (378 yards) and the 3rd (385 yards) on several occasions. Similarly, the 19th hole at the Cork Golf Club comes alive in animated recall of their man driving the 6th (321 yards), the 8th (332 yards) and the uphill 16th (274 yards). The story goes that Bruen would then go down to the modesty of a mere three wood to drive the green at both the 3rd (274 yards) and the 12th (268 yards).

At the Home International matches in Portmarnock in 1949, a driving competition was held in which all the players in the Irish, English, Scottish and Welsh teams competed. The carry achieved was measured and the longest recorded was 280 yards, by Bruen.

Joe Carr, three times winner of the British Amateur Championship and an inspiration to all Irish golfers.

In May 1938, taking part in trials at St Andrews for the selection of the British and Irish Walker Cup team, Bruen, on his opening reconnaissance around the Old Course, returned a 71 and repeated it — and followed that up with a 68 and a 72. It was a startling performance of which Henry Cotton wrote: 'Fancy a 17-year-old doing 282 in four rounds on the Old Lady of St Andrews. I know what a stern course it is, long, difficult and tricky; but here was a mere boy playing it with a wise head and a technique which left everyone gasping. I have not known a player to do such scores no matter what his age. This boy Bruen has set a standard for all players.'

When the Irish marvel shot two 69s to lead the qualifiers into the 1939 British Open at St Andrews, the eyes of the sporting world were riveted on him in anticipation. Unfortunately, the brilliant Irish youth could not maintain this scorching form and he eventually finished eight shots behind the winner, Richard (Dick) Burton, though noted critics of the day rated Bruen as the best player in the field.

Winner of the British Amateur Championship in 1946, the Irish Close Championship in 1937 and 1938, the Irish Amateur Open in 1938, and three times a Walker Cup player, the high esteem in which Bruen was held was recalled by Joe Carr. 'In Ireland, Jimmy Bruen set the standard from which the rest of us benefited. He was one of the all-time great golfers — and a particularly nice fellow.'

Jimmy Bruen died in 1972; he was only five days short of his 52nd birthday.

That Bruen truly lit the flame of achievement for Irish golfers abroad was evidenced quickly and comprehensively as they entered the post World War II era that truly established Irish golf — and its golfers — in the international shop window of the game.

Eleven years after Bruen's milestone deed at Royal Birkdale, Fred Daly won the British Open title at Hoylake. In 1949 Harry Bradshaw tied for the British Open. Starting in 1953, Joe Carr won the British Amateur Championship three times. In 1958 Harry Bradshaw and Christy O'Connor won the Canada (now World) Cup tournament for Ireland in Mexico City. The same two players won the Masters twice each between 1953 and 1959. In 1965 Ireland won the first of two successive Amateur European Cups, and in 1970 O'Connor established a record when he won the then richest ever individual prize in world golf — £25,000 sterling — in the John Player Classic.

Christy O'Connor, Snr, executes an extraordinary bunker recovery while playing with the Scot, Eric Brown, in the 1957 Ryder Cup at Lindrick and with J. C. Snead during the Ryder Cup match at Muirfield in 1973.

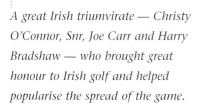

A great Irish triumvirate — Christy O'Connor, Snr, Joe Carr and Harry Bradshaw — who brought great honour to Irish golf and helped popularise the spread of the game.

Even if the general standard has never quite reached the same lofty heights, the lady golfers were also playing a critical role in the growth and image of golf in Ireland. That contribution, as we have seen, began with the exploits of May Hezlet and Rhona Adair and was strengthened by such other well-known exponents as Clarrie Reddan neé Tiernan, Kitty MacCann, Philomena Garvey, Mary McKenna and Claire Hourihane.

A contradiction, when it comes to assessing the merits of Irish golfers, is that Fred Daly's Open triumph of 1947 endures in isolation. Indeed, 'Whistling' Fred might have rectified that imbalance himself, since he was runner-up to his great rival, Henry Cotton, in 1948, and he finished third to another of his great adversaries, Bobby Locke, in both 1950 and 1952.

Fred Daly, who pointed the way for following generations, lifted shoulder high by well wishers following his triumph in the British Open at Hoylake in 1947, and with Gene Sarazen in 1970.

The harrowing manner in which Harry Bradshaw lost the British Open Championship at Royal St George's in 1949 has become part of golf's rich folklore.

At the 5th hole, in the second round, the Brad, after his second shot, found the ball lodged inside the broken shoulder of a bottle, with the neck and sharp points sticking up.

Much fiction has been written about the incident, even about the precise identity of the bottle and its original contents!

How a bottle could come to be in the line of fire during an Open Championship was outlined in a report which stated: 'The green at the 5th hole is close to the shingle beach and someone who had been having an alfresco lunch had carelessly tossed an empty bottle, whose contents had been made not a hundred miles from Bradshaw's Kilcroney Club, on to the course.'

Gallant Harry Bradshaw and Bobby Locke at the prize-giving ceremony following the 1949 British Open in which the Irishman was the victim of an infamous 'beer bottle' incident.

Another extravagant account added rich irony to the Irishman's dilemma by a similar suggestion that the blame lay in the bosom of a Guinness bottle, adding: 'Somebody had thrown away a bottle, whose label would puzzle nobody on the streets of Dublin!'

It all served to embellish the fabled tale but, had the bemused Irishman treated the ball as an unplayable lie, he might have been involved in a disqualification — as a result, the rule was changed permitting a free drop — so he decided to play it as it lay.

With his 'blaster' — a 9 iron equivalent — Bradshaw shut his eyes, turned his head away and blindly swung at the bottle. He made good contact as he smashed the glass into smithereens and sent the ball about 30 feet. The hole, a par 4, cost him a 6, and after four rounds he tied with South Africa's Bobby Locke on 283, which equalled the lowest total since the championship was extended to 72 holes in 1892.

Compared to such drama, the play-off the next day was an anticlimax. The Irishman ran into Bobby Locke at his most devastating, and rounds of 67 and 68 against 74 and 73 compounded Bradshaw's misery.

As an attempted means of exorcising the incident from his mind, Harry later gave the ball away to a friend. But the controversy lingers on.

As well as being unquestionably one of the finest post-war players (he was the first Irishman to win the Irish Open, in 1946; he was Ireland's first Ryder Cup player, in 1947; and he was twice British Match Play champion), Fred's genial nature also established him as one of the great personalities. As he stomped the fairways the man who learned his golf on the great links of Royal Portrush stood out for his distinctive jaunty walk, his rolling gait, his tuneful whistling, and also the idiosyncrasy of taking an interminable number of waggles before playing a shot.

The Bobby Jones Award presented to Joe Carr in 1961. The award is given in recognition of distinguished sportsmanship in golf and is presented by the United States Golf Association to commemorate the contributions to the cause of fair play made by Robert (Bobby) Tyre Jones Jnr.

It was unfortunate that his partner, Harry Bradshaw, was not to emulate the feat of being crowned Open champion.

The infamous incident of the broken beer bottle at Royal St George's in 1949 has been consigned to sporting history as one of the most bizarre. The cruel manner in which the Brad was restricted to a tie for the title after seventy-two holes alongside Bobby Locke could not happen today, as Bradshaw's fate was to bring about a change in the rules. Genial Harry, however, never let his misfortune affect his happy-go-lucky disposition. If anything, he was apt to embroider the legend when asked about it and, as with all his stories, one was all the better for having heard it in his company.

Legion were the numbers who made the pilgrimage to Portmarnock, where he was the popular professional for over thirty years, just to shake the hand of a renowned ambassador, whose no-frills-attached three-quarter swing and personalised 'rap-and-listen-for-the-drop' putting style made him as famous on the fairways as his many great triumphs.

Most notable perhaps in a portfolio boasting two Dunlop Masters titles, a PGA Championship title, two Irish Open titles, ten Irish National PGA titles and significant involvement in the Ryder Cup teams of 1953, 1955 and 1957 (winners), was his

Happier times: Harry Bradshaw and Christy O'Connor receive the Canada Cup for Ireland in Mexico City, 1958.

performance in single-handedly leading Ireland to a historic victory in the Canada Cup in Mexico city in 1958.

Christy O'Connor was his partner, but has always contended: 'But for Harry we would never have won it.' Rounds of 70-70-76-70 outline the Brad's dominance against 73-73-74-73 by O'Connor.

Famous Irish amateur players: (from left) Joe Carr, Cecil Ewing, Charles Hezlet, Jimmy Bruen and John Burke.

The high altitude and spongy underfoot conditions in the mile-high city caused many players great distress. Some were left gasping for breath. The rotund Irishman's gait among the thirty-two competing nations suggested he might be a victim of the tough conditions. Courageously, he defied the odds to lead Ireland to a three stroke win over Spain. Regrettably, there was yet again to be a tinge of sadness about the occasion, because Harry lost a sudden-death play-off for the individual trophy when Angel Miguel of Spain holed a 25 foot birdie putt at the 3rd extra hole.

O'Connor, or Himself as he was more affectionately known, formed another great golfing triumvirate with Daly and Bradshaw. The argument endures as to who was the best. Suffice to say each carved his own niche and left the game with a rich legacy, though in O'Connor's case it will ever remain a cruel

irony that he did not win a British Open.

A tie for third place in 1958 and 1961 and a shared runner-up finish to Peter Thomson in 1965 stand as an everlasting testament to how close the Galway farmer's son came to being crowned champion. His near miss at Royal Lytham and St Anne's in 1958 is chronicled as his closest call. On the 72nd tee, the Irishman, famed for his graceful, rhythmic swing, required a birdie three to win — or a par 4 for a tie. The maestro from Royal Dublin had played immediately behind Thomson for the previous two rounds (played on the same day) and had filed a complaint against the Australian's slow pace of play, which O'Connor felt was an intentional ploy.

In the event, the distracted Irishman's composure was certainly not helped by the inability of the hard-pressed stewards to marshal the thronging crowds, who were desperate to see if the Irishman and his Argentinian partner, Leopoldo Ruiz, could match the score of Thomson and Dave Thomas of Wales who were sharing the lead in the clubhouse.

Ten disruptive minutes passed while the final pairing on the course waited impatiently as stewards and police attempted to clear the 18th fairway so that play could continue. It was a hopeless scene and finally, as there seemed no option but to resume, there was only half the target to aim at as the huge crowd broke rank and swallowed up the right-hand side of the fairway.

'Great shot, Christy,' roared someone, after the Irishman hit a three wood instead of his driver in a tactical ploy to avoid the left-hand bunkers which had been brought more sharply into play because of the crowds.

'You judged it perfectly,' his supporters reassured him.

So, one can imagine how Christy's pounding heart sank when he jostled his way through the bedlam, only to discover that his ball was imbedded in the sand! With the green 160 yards away — and O'Connor's partner leaving his ball in the same bunker after taking the gamble of trying for the green — there was no option but to play safely out and hope to retrieve the situation by at best chipping into the hole or at least getting down with a chip and a putt.

It was not to be!

The pitch-and-run third shot ran on fifteen feet past the hole, and the return putt to save the Open stopped on the lip. All had been lost.

When it was said to him that the great Henry Cotton had declared Fred Daly to be Ireland's greatest ever golfer simply because he won a British Open title, O'Connor retorted with a trenchant rebuff that will forever fuel the 19th hole debate.

'The consistent winning of major tournaments over a long period of time, as in my three decades, might be adjudged to be of greater merit than hitting the jackpot once'.

It is a reasonable point, taking account of a career enhanced by his ten Ryder Cup appearances, ten Irish PGA titles, twenty-one outright British and Irish circuit wins, including two Masters titles, one PGA Match Play Championship and countless other victories on the domestic scene.

Certainly, O'Connor's victories in the Carroll's tournaments during the heady days of the 1960s and 70s were instrumental in popularising the game of golf in Ireland. So was the manner of his victory in the Dunlop Masters tournament, staged with such success at Portmarnock in September 1959.

The name of Joe Carr was on every golfer's lips during the 1950s and 60s as he won

Between the 3rd and the 13th fairways of the Royal Dublin Golf Club, and surrounded by a high stone wall enclosing Curley's Yard, is a derelict one-roomed cottage with a red tin roof. The adjacent 15th hole is known as Moran's and therein lies a clue to the cottage-owned by one of the most famous personalities in Irish golf.

Michael Moran was born there in 1886, becoming part of golfing folklore as the man who gave the term 'dyke' to the Irish golfing lexicon.

The story goes that as a caddy he was not permitted to play on the links but, stealthily playing from within the drainage dykes on the course, he became fondly known as Dyke Moran, the word 'dyke' meaning a birdie in the terminology of today.

Dyke Moran went on to become virtually unbeatable in Ireland as he won the Irish Professional Championship in every year from 1909 through to 1913. In 1913 he seemed destined to earn world fame when he finished in a tie for third place in the British Open, held at Hoylake, while competing with a set of borrowed clubs and wearing army boots!

Tragically he died, aged 32, when he was wounded in the Great War. He passed away at Le Gateau in December 1918, one month after peace had been signed.

almost everything available to him — and many times over!

J. B., as he was affectionately called, had a distinctive, flailing action, a frequent wayward length, yet a peerless reputation as a genius of improvisation, ever capable of reversing a dangerous situation with a devastating shot or a brilliant recovery.

This magical gift, married to a steely determination that would not accept the notion of defeat until it became absolute, placed him consistently beyond his peers and into a position whereby we are left to ponder what might have been, had he turned professional.

Although the son of the club steward at Portmarnock Golf Club, he represented his beloved nine hole Sutton Club across the estuary and revelled in the cut and thrust of match play.

Michael 'Dyke' Moran.

Globe trotting Ronan Rafferty high among the Swiss Alps . . .

. . . and negotiating the final hole at the Emirates Golf Club in Dubai.

*Trouble shooter
Padraig Harrington
demonstrates his
ability to extricate
himself safely from
hazards.*

If there is a tendency in Ireland to assess the merits of all our players against those who went before them, Garth McGimpsey need have no qualms. His reputation is such that he is admired by today's generation of players as 'the Legend'.

A winner of the British Amateur Championship and twice the Irish champion, the merit of the determined Ulsterman, a product of the Bangor Club, is that he has also won all but the South of Ireland title in a championship haul that reached thirteen, with victory at 40 years of age and for the third time in the 1996 West of Ireland Championship.

More than that, McGimpsey has represented Ireland with distinction well in excess of 100 times. He has also played in three Walker Cup teams, most notably at Peachtree in 1989 when he contributed an invaluable 1½ points to Britain and Ireland's famous win.

Pride of place must be his British title win in 1985, beating Graham Homewood of England at Royal Dornoch, one of the great if remote and therefore underplayed, links of Scotland.

A measure of McGimpsey's achievement at 29 years of age was that he reached the final without being taken past the 16th green, and in the thirty-six hole decider he crushed his final opponent by 8 and 7!

It was entirely fitting that his margin of victory should be precisely the same as that by Joe Carr, the last Irishman to win twenty-five years previously when he beat Bob Cochran of the USA.

Mc Gimpsey had also become the first Ulsterman to ascend this golfing peak since Max McCready beat Willie (the Wedge) Turnesa, one of the famous seven golfing brothers from the USA, by 2 and 1 at Portmarnock in 1949.

Man-to-man combat was his forte, as three British Amateur titles (1953, 1958 and 1960), a record stint of ten Walker Cup appearances between 1947 and 1967, five Irish Amateur titles and twenty-nine other Provincial or Irish Open wins, will illustrate. But he also excelled at stroke play, invariably driven by the ambition in 'peg the pros', as he would mischievously declare. He did once, beating the best of Ireland (excepting Christy O'Connor) to win the Southern PGA title at Milltown in 1967.

On more illustrious occasions, too, he also shaped as if he was about to beat the pros. One unforgettable example was the Dunlop Masters at Portmarnock in 1959.

As the kingpin amateur of Europe, J. B. was invited to be the only non-professional in a field of twenty-five. It was a challenge that the swashbuckling Carr relished as, being born and bred on the links, he knew the course quite literally like the back of his hand. Duly, he made his mark and was the only player to break 70 twice on the first day. His 68 followed by 69 against the par of 74 gave him a tie for the halfway lead with Bernard Hunt's 67–70.

In those days seventy-two holes were played over two days and when J. B. started the last day by holing a shot from fully 100 yards range for an eagle 2 at the 3rd hole, the omens seemed to be that, indeed, the professionals were about to be beaten and that Carr would carve a famous victory and confirm his standing as one of the world's greatest amateur players.

Garth McGimpsey — a legend!

At lunchtime, after a third round 69, his aggregate score stood at 206. That gave him a four shot advantage over Christy O'Connor, Snr, with hardened British circuit stalwarts John Panton, Dai Rees, Eric Brown and Bernard Hunt a shot further back. It did seem as if the pros were about to be pegged!

Typically, however, O'Connor had his own plan. He was playing five two-balls ahead of Carr and he reckoned if he was to have any chance of catching the leader, he needed to get to work early and hope that the news filtering back down the grapevine would cause his great rival to worry. The plan worked. O'Connor scored 4-3-4-4-3-4 over the first six holes against the par of 4-4-4-5-4-5, while Carr started out 4-5-4-4-4-6. Not only had Carr's lead been wiped out; O'Connor was now in front.

For once, O'Connor was in complete harmony with his putter and, going on to play what he later described as 'the best round of my life' (he was barely five years on the circuit), he finished with 66 for 276. It gave him a four-shot cushion on what was truly a proud day for Ireland. Carr slipped to 74 but, none the less, he had a tremendous run and he tied with Norman Drew, who finished with a 68, for second place: an Irish 1-2-3 on an occasion also marked by a huge attendance as an enthusiastic Irish gallery demonstrated its love for the big occasion and golf's vibrant new image.

On another occasion, Carr was rubbing shoulders with the leaders after an opening salvo of 3-4-4 in the final round of the British Open at St Andrews in 1960, only for rain to cause a cancellation just as the redoubtable Irish amateur was within sight of the ultimate crowning glory.

When recalling the acclaim achieved by Bruen, Daly, Bradshaw, O'Connor and Carr in that golden era for Irish golf throughout the 40s, 50s, 60s and 70s, one gains a fair measure of the glory in which Irish golf basked. Yet, the story of Ireland's achievements is not confined to them.

Cecil Ewing was also a household name, a colossus, winning the West of Ireland at his beloved Rosses Point on ten occasions and making a handsome contribution to Ireland and the Walker Cup.

John Burke, who also played in the Walker Cup, similarly lorded the fairways. Eight times the Irish champion, the Lahinch legend so dominated the South of Ireland Championship that he was eventually asked not to enter for fear of frightening away the opposition, thereby threatening the economic life of the famous holiday village of Lahinch!

Des Smith who put in a brave performance at the Open Championship at Troon in 1982.

Challenging times —
at Ardglass . . .

. . . Armagh

. . . and Portstewart.

In any event, he triumphed eleven times from 1928, failing for a twelfth and sixth successive time in 1947 when he lost in an epic final to the renowned Brud Slattery.

That David Sheahan, a 21-year-old medical student, could go out and spread-eagle a star-cast field of professionals to win the Jeyes Tournament at Royal Dublin in 1962 at much the same time as Tom Craddock's career was similarly beginning to blossom, demonstrated in heartening fashion how the line of great players was being continued.

The achievements of the late Pat Mulcare, Ronan Rafferty, Philip Walton, Arthur Pierse, Garth McGimpsey, John McHenry, Raymond Burns and Jody Fanagan, in more recent times, further emphasises the point that under the caring guidance of the Golfing Union of Ireland any emerging talent in Irish amateur golf will be guided on the right path.

Two sides of David Feherty — player and commentator.

As the previously confined British and Irish professional circuit was then beginning to make strides in a European context, Ireland's continuing role in the forefront of affairs was also assured.

Eamonn Darcy, one of Ireland's stalwart professionals, whose exploits in the 1987 Ryder Cup at Muirfield Village, Ohio, were acknowledged by United States captain Jack Nicklaus as the backbone of Europe's historic first victory on American soil.

It remains a disappointment that none of the younger players has been able to reach that step further up the ladder to major winner's status, but there is no lack of determination. The heavens above Woodbrook and Portmarnock still ring out with the emotional salutes accorded Christy O'Connor, Jnr, in 1975 and John O'Leary in 1982 when they followed in the footsteps of Daly and Bradshaw as Irish Open winners.

In an era when the quality of professional golf has never been greater, these achievements and the many more won around the world by the present generation have all served to consolidate Ireland's honoured place in the game.

The heights attained by Darcy, when getting up and down from a greenside bunker to beat Ben Crenshaw at Muirfield Village in 1987 and lauded by US team captain Jack Nicklaus as the single most critical act in achieving a historic victory for Europe; the fabled two iron shot by O'Connor, Jnr, over the lake at the Belfry's dramatic 18th hole to establish victory over Fred Couples which ensured that Europe would keep the trophy in 1989; and then Philip Walton's contribution in taking the match-deciding point from Jay Haas at Oak Hill Country Club, New York, in 1995, serve to confirm the point that the continuing well-being of Irish golf is in safe hands.

Team-mates salute Philip Walton on his 18th hole victory over American Jay Haas to clinch victory for Europe in the dramatic climax to the 1995 Ryder Cup at Oak Hill Country Club, New York.

GREAT MOMENTS IN IRISH GOLF

1891 Golfing Union of Ireland formed in the Royal Hotel, Belfast, on 13 November; on 13 May the first ever competition for ladies in Irish golf took place at the Killymoon Club, called the Killymoon Golf Club's Ladies' Scratch Medal.

The medals presented in Belfast Golf Club, 1881, for members and associates monthly handicap competitions at Holywood. These were the first golf prizes ever competed for in Ireland.

1892 Alexander Stuart of the Honourable Company of Edinburgh Golfers became the first player to be crowned champion of Ireland when beating fellow Scot, J. H. Andrew, by two holes in the final of the inaugural Irish Amateur Open Championship at Portrush.

1893 Irish Ladies' Golf Union formed on 15 December in the Girls' Friendly Society, Belfast.

1894 Handicap system, devised by George Combe, adopted as first ever in Ireland; Miss Clara Mulligan won inaugural Irish Women's Close Championship at Carnalea.

1895 First professional tournament ever held in Ireland, staged at Portrush, in match play format, won by Alexander (Sandy) Herd, who beat Harry Vardon; South of Ireland Championship inaugurated at Lahinch, becoming the first of the provincial championships; Portrush nominated as first links outside England to house the British Ladies' Championship, won by Lady Margaret Scott.

1896 First interprovincial match played, at Portrush.

Alexander (Sandy) Herd, winner of the first ever professional tournament staged in Ireland, at Portrush, 1895, seen here on the 9th green, also at Portrush, in another match, against Ben Sayers, 1898.

1899 Miss May Hezlet becomes first Irish golfer ever to win British title in the Ladies' British Open Amateur Championship, Newcastle, Co. Down, in the week of her 17th birthday. It was the first of three such triumphs.

1905 Henry Boyd becomes first Irish player to win Irish Amateur Open Championship, defeating J. F. Mitchell at Royal Dublin.

Jimmy Bruen (left), Cecil Ewing and Henry Cotton setting off on a practice round prior to the Walker Cup at St Andrews, 1938. Britain and Ireland went on to win the title for the first time.

1907 Ireland won the Home International Ladies' Championship for first time, at Newcastle, Co. Down; this represented the first win by an Irish team in international competition.

1909 Lionel Munn ends dominance by overseas players in Irish Amateur Open by winning first of a hat-trick at Royal Dublin.

1924 Charles Hezlet becomes first Irishman to be picked for the Walker Cup team.

1927 First ever Irish Open Championship staged at Portmarnock, won by George Duncan.

1934 Mrs J. B. (Pat) Walker becomes first Irish player picked for Curtis Cup match.

1936 Jimmy Bruen wins British Boys' Championship at Royal Birkdale, becoming first Irishman to win major British title.

1938 Cecil Ewing and Jimmy Bruen play on first ever winning British and Irish Walker Cup team, at St Andrews.

1946 Belfast-born Jimmy Bruen becomes first Irishman to win the British Amateur Championship, at Royal Birkdale; Philomena Garvey wins first of record fifteen Irish Women's Close Championship titles; Fred Daly wins the Irish Open at Portmarnock.

1947 Fred Daly becomes first Irishman to win British Open Championship at Hoylake, Liverpool; Harry Bradshaw wins Irish Open at Royal Portrush; Fred Daly wins PGA Match Play Championship at Royal Lytham and St Anne's; Joe Carr selected for first Walker Cup match, subsequently set record of ten appearances to 1967.

1948 Fred Daly wins Penfold Tournament at Gleneagles; Fred Daly wins PGA Match Play Championship at Birkdale.

1949 Harry Bradshaw ties with Bobby Locke in British Open Championship at Royal St George's, Sandwich, but loses play-off; Max McCready wins only British Amateur Championship held in Republic of Ireland; McCready, Joe Carr, Cecil Ewing and Jimmy Bruen selected on British and Irish Walker Cup team, an Irish record number to this day; Harry Bradshaw wins Irish Open at Belvoir Park.

WINNING GOLF By BYRON NELSON

GOLF
ILLUSTRATED

No. 1990 Established 1890. Thursday, October 30, 1947 Weekly, One Shilling

OUR RYDER CUP TEAM IN LIGHT-HEARTED MOOD ABOARD THE QUEEN MARY

SUBSCRIPTION RATES : Inland and Abroad £3 3s. per annum. Canada £3 per annum including postage. 15

The front cover of Golf Illustrated, *30 October 1947, showing Fred Daly, the first Irishman to be selected for the Ryder Cup, getting in some practice on board the Queen Mary as the British and Irish team was travelling to the USA.*

1950 John Glover wins British Boys' Championship at Royal Lytham and St Anne's.

1951 Fred Daly becomes first ever Irishman selected for the Ryder Cup team; British Open Championship played in Ireland for the only time — Max Faulkner winning at Royal Portrush; Mrs Kitty MacCann becomes first post-war British Amateur Open Champion from Ireland at Broadstone.

1952 Philomena Garvey selected on first ever British and Irish team to win Curtis Cup, at Muirfield. Mrs Kitty MacCann was a member of the team, but did not play due to illness; Fred Daly wins Daks Golf Tournament at Wentworth; Fred Daly wins PGA Match Play Championship at Walton Heath.

John Glover, British champion boy golfer, 1950.

Ireland's greatest post-war lady golfer, Philomena Garvey, who won the first of her record fifteen Irish Women's Close Championship titles in 1946.

Hickory-shafted putter presented in 1978 to Portmarnock Golf Club by Dr P. J. Hillery, President of Ireland, which hangs in the members' bar and is played for each year in foursome competition.

History-maker Norman Drew, who played in the Walker, Ryder and Canada Cup.

1953 Joe Carr becomes the first player born in the Republic of Ireland to win British Amateur Championship, at Hoylake, Liverpool, winning again in 1958 at St Andrews and in 1960 at Royal Portrush; Harry Bradshaw becomes first player from the Republic of Ireland to play in the Ryder Cup; Harry Bradshaw wins British (Dunlop) Masters at Sunningdale.

1954 Baba Beck becomes the first Irish person to captain a British and Irish team in the Curtis Cup, with Daisy Ferguson (1958), Maire O'Donnell (1982) and Ita Butler (1996) following in her footsteps.

1955 Christy O'Connor, Snr, becomes first player in European golf to win four-figure cheque (£1,000) when taking Swallow Penfold Tournament at Llandudno, Wales; Harry Bradshaw wins British (Dunlop) Masters at Little Aston; Christy O'Connor, Snr, plays in first of record ten Ryder Cup matches.

1956 Christy O'Connor, Snr, wins British (Dunlop) Masters at Prestwick.

1957 Philomena Garvey, a finalist also in 1946, 1953, 1960 and 1963, wins Ladies' British Amateur Open title at Gleneagles; Christy O'Connor, Snr, wins PGA Match Play Championship at Turnberry.

1958 Harry Bradshaw and Christy O'Connor, Snr, win Canada (World) Cup in Mexico city, becoming first European nation to take the title; Bradshaw ties for Individual Championship, loses in play-off; Harry Bradshaw wins PGA Championship at Llandudno.

1959 Christy O'Connor, Snr, wins British (Dunlop) Masters at Portmarnock; Christy O'Connor, Snr, wins Daks Golf Tournament at Wentworth; Norman Drew wins Yorkshire Evening News Tournament.

1960 Norman Drew becomes first Irish golfer ever to play in Walker Cup (1953), Ryder Cup (1959) and Canada (World) Cup (1960); Canada (World) Cup staged in Ireland for only time, at Portmarnock; Christy O'Connor, Snr, wins Irish Hospitals Tournament at Woodbrook.

1965 Ireland wins European Amateur Team Championship for first time, at Royal St George's, Sandwich.

Welcome home . . . Christy O'Connor, Snr, then attached to Killarney Golf Club, salutes the crowds lining the streets to welcome him back after he and Harry Bradshaw won the Canada Cup for Ireland in Mexico City, 1958.

Golf equipment as it would have been in Ireland in times long past: the making of a feathery ball and a selection of old clubs and balls.

Hidden gems — at Blainroe . . .

. . . North West

. . . and Clonmel.

1962 Amateur David Sheahan wins Jeyes Professional-Amateur Tournament at Royal Dublin; Christy O'Connor, Snr, wins Irish Hospitals Tournament at Woodbrook.

1963 P. J. Carroll and Co. enter professional tournament golf sponsorship for first time, at Woodbrook, with Carroll's Sweet Afton Tournament (won by Bernard Hunt), leading to revival of the Irish Open Championship in 1975.

1964 Christy O'Connor, Snr, wins Carroll's Sweet Afton Tournament at Woodbrook; Christy O'Connor, Snr, wins Martini International at Wentworth; Christy O'Connor, Snr, wins Jeyes Professional-Amateur Tournament at Cork (Little Island).

1966 Christy O'Connor, Snr, wins Carroll's International at Royal Dublin, finishing eagle-birdie-eagle; Hugh Boyle wins Daks Golf Tournament at Wentworth; Christy O'Connor, Snr, wins Gallaher Ulster Open at Shandon Park.

1967 Ireland wins European Amateur Team Championship for second time, at Circolo Club, Turin, Italy; Christy O'Connor, Snr, wins Carroll's International at Woodbrook.

1968 Carol Wallace becomes first Irish player to win British Girls' Championship, at Leven; Jimmy Martin wins Carroll's International at Woodbrook; Christy O'Connor, Snr, wins Gallaher Ulster Open at Shandon Park.

Roddy Carr, who made history at St Andrews in 1971 by following his father Joe as a Walker Cup player. They are the only father and son pairing to be so honoured.

1969 Christy O'Connor, Snr, wins Gallaher Ulster Open at Shandon Park.

1970 Christy O'Connor, Snr, wins richest first prize in world golf — £25,000 in John Player Classic at Notts Golf Club, Hollinwell; Mary McKenna selected for first of record nine Curtis Cup matches; Paddy Skerritt wins Alcan Tournament at Portmarnock.

1971 Roddy Carr makes history by following his father, Joe, as a Walker Cup player, at St Andrews, the only father and son pairing to be so honoured. Carr, Jnr, undefeated as Britain and Ireland win match for first time since 1938; Josephine Mark wins British Girls'

Championship at North Berwick; Eddie Polland wins Parmeco Golf Classic at Rushcliffe; Ernie Jones wins Kenya Open at Muthaiga.

John O'Leary, who made his professional tournament winning breakthrough in 1975.

1972 Christy O'Connor, Snr, wins Carroll's International at Woodbrook; Jimmy Kinsella wins Madrid Open at Puerta de Hierro.

1973 Paddy McGuirk wins Carroll's International at Woodbrook; Eddie Polland wins Swallow Penfold Tournament at Queen's Park.

1974 Liam Higgins wins Kerrygold International Classic at Waterville; Christy O'Connor, Jnr, wins Zambian Open.

1975 Irish Open Championship revived at Woodbrook, won by Christy O'Connor, Jnr; Eddie Polland wins PGA Match Play Championship at Lindrick; John O'Leary wins Sumrie Better Ball Tournament, with Jack Newton, at Queen's Park; John O'Leary wins South African Holiday Inns Tournament.

1976 Eddie Polland wins Spanish Open at La Manga; Eamonn Darcy wins World Under 25s Championship at Evian, France; John O'Leary wins Greater Manchester Open at Wilmslow; Eamonn Darcy and Christy O'Connor, Jnr, win Sumrie Better Ball Tournament at Queen's Park; Christy O'Connor, Snr, wins first of record six (also 1977, 1979, 1981, 1982, 1983) PGA Seniors Open Championships at North Berwick; Christy O'Connor, Snr, wins first of two (also 1977) World Seniors Professional Championships at Whitecraigs, Scotland.

1977 Eamonn Darcy wins Greater Manchester Open at Wilmslow; Liam Higgins wins Kerrygold International Classic at Waterville; Liam Higgins wins Kenya Open at Muthaiga.

1978 Eamonn Darcy and Christy O'Connor, Jnr, win Sumrie Better Ball Tournament at Queen's Park; Paddy Skerritt wins first of two PGA Seniors Open Championships (also 1980) at Cambridgeshire.

1979 Maureen Madill wins the British Amateur Championship title at Nairn; Ronan Rafferty wins British Boys' Championship at Barassie; Ireland wins European Women's Team Championship for first time, at Hermitage; Mary McKenna wins Ladies' British Open Amateur Stroke Play Championship at Moseley; Des Smyth wins PGA Match Play Championship at Fulford.

Popular Paddy Skerritt, winner of the Alcan Tournament in 1970.

1980 Ireland wins Ladies' Home International Championship for first time since 1907, at Cruden Bay; Mary McKenna, Claire Nesbitt, Maureen Madill selected on British and Irish Curtis Cup team, Ireland's biggest ever representation at the time; Maureen Madill wins British Open Amateur Stroke Play Championship at Brancepeth Castle; Ronan Rafferty ties with Peter McEvoy for English Open Amateur Stroke Play Championship (Brabazon Trophy) at Hunstanton, aged 16 years and 4 months; Eddie Polland wins Spanish Open at Escorpion; Des Smyth wins Greater Manchester Open at Wilmslow; Des Smyth wins Newcastle Brown '900' Open at Northumberland; Des Smyth wins Welsh Golf Classic at Royal Porthcawl; Eamonn Darcy wins Air New Zealand Open; Ronan Rafferty becomes youngest ever winner of the Irish Amateur Championship, aged 16 years and 7 months.

1981 Eamonn Darcy wins Australian West Lakes Classic; Philip Walton wins Spanish Amateur Open Championship; Philip Walton wins Scottish Amateur Open Strokes Championship at Erskine and Renfrew.

1982 John O'Leary becomes fourth Irishman, after Fred Daly, Harry Bradshaw and Christy O'Connor, Jnr, to win the Irish Open at Portmarnock; Ronan Rafferty wins Venezuelan Open; Eamonn Darcy wins Kenya Open at Muthaiga.

1983 Unprecedented European Amateur Team Championship double by Ireland's men and women teams on same day at Chantilly, France, and Waterloo, Brussels, respectively;

Mrs. J. M. HULTON
GOODARDS
STEEPLE ASHTON
NR. TROWBRIDGE
WILTS.
Tel. Keevil (038067) 315

14th Sept.

Dear Miss Madill
Just a line to say I am delighted at Ireland winning the Home Internationals I send my congratulations to you & all the team. 72 years ago since Ireland won. I think it was the last time Mrs Ross captained the team & she & I both played in it. With all the best of luck to future triumphs
Yours sincerely
Violet Hulton (nee Hezlet)

Letter sent to Maureen Madill when Ireland won the Ladies' Home International Championship for first time since 1907, at Cruden Bay, Scotland. It came from Violet Hezlet who had played in 1907.

Ballybunion Golf Club

MEN'S CARD   SSS 72 70 68

COMPETITION ....
DATE 8 - 7 - 81. TIME ....

PLAYER **A** .... TOM WATSON .... Handicap............ Strokes from Par............

PLAYER **B** .... Handicap............ Strokes from Par............

Hole	C'ship Metres (Blue)	Medal Metres (White)	Forward Metres (Green)	Par	Strokes Index	A	B	O +/-	Hole	C'ship Metres (Blue)	Medal Metres (White)	Forward Metres (Green)	Par	Strokes Index	A	B	O +/-
1	358	337	299	4	9	4			10	326	304	276	4	10	4		
2	397	367	339	4	1	5			11	405	361	349	4	2	4		
3	198	196	168	3	11	3			12	169	166	151	3	16	3		
4	461	459	449	5	15	4			13	443	441	438	5	8	5		
5	465	453	435	5	13	5			14	126	123	113	3	18	3		
6	333	312	294	4	7	4			15	208	201	199	3	4	3		
7	407	404	351	4	5	4			16	442	439	422	5	14	4		
8	138	135	114	3	17	3			17	357	343	321	4	12	5		
9	416	384	367	4	3	4			18	348	344	330	4	6	4		
Out	3173	3047	2816	36		36			In	2824	2722	2599	35		35		
									Out	3173	3047	2816	36		36		
									Total	5997	5769	5415	71		71		

Marker's Signature ... Sandy Tatum

Player's Signature ... Tom Watson

Holes won		Handicap	
Holes lost		Nett Score	
Result			

To convert metres into yards divide metres by ten and add to original figure. e.g. 358—10 = 36 + 358 = 394 yards.

Card recorded by Tom Watson on his first visit to Ballybunion in 1981. The marker's signature is that of Sandy Tatum, who was instrumental in bringing the five times British Open champion to Ballybunion, where Watson has carried out design alterations to the famous Old Course.

Eamonn Darcy wins Spanish Open at Las Brisas; Des Smyth wins Sanyo Open at El Prat; Claire Hourihane wins South Atlantic Tournament, USA.

457; Gerry Costello wins British Ladies' Senior Open Stroke Play Championship at Prestatyn, Wales; Ernie Jones wins PGA Seniors Open Championship at Stratford-on-Avon.

1986 Ireland wins the Ladies' Home International Championship at Whittington Barracks; Mary McKenna, Claire Hourihane and Lillian Behan selected for winning British and Irish team in Curtis Cup match at Prairie Dunes, Kansas, the first occasion that a visiting team beat America in a Curtis Cup, Walker Cup or Ryder Cup match; Claire Hourihane wins Ladies' British Open Amateur Stroke Play Championship at Blairgowrie; David Feherty wins Italian Open at Albarella, Venice; David Feherty wins Scottish Open at Haggs Castle; Leslie Walker wins British Boys' Championship at Seaton Carew.

Historic double — Garth McGimpsey and Lillian Behan, winners of the Men's and Ladies' British Amateur Open Championships in 1985.

1984 David Feherty wins South African ICL International.

1985 Lillian Behan wins Ladies' British Amateur Open at Ganton, Yorkshire; Garth McGimpsey wins British Amateur Championship at Royal Dornoch, Scotland, from an entry of

Defiant Eamonn Darcy, after holing the decisive putt that earned Europe victory in the Ryder Cup at Muirfield Village, Ohio, 1987.

1987 Ireland wins Triple Crown for first time ever in Men's Home International Championship at Lahinch, captained by Eamon Curran; Eamonn Darcy wins Belgian Open at Waterloo; Ronan Rafferty wins South Australian Open; Ronan Rafferty wins New Zealand Open; Michael Quirke wins Spanish Amateur Open Championship; Claire Hourihane wins Spanish Ladies' Open Amateur Championship.

1988 Des Smyth wins Jersey Open at La Moye; Ronan Rafferty wins Italian Open, at Monticello; Ireland (Des Smyth, Ronan Rafferty, Eamonn Darcy) wins Dunhill Nations Cup for first time, at St Andrews; Ronan Rafferty wins Equity and Law Challenge at Royal Mid-Surrey; David Feherty wins South African Lexington PGA Championship; Ronan Rafferty wins Australian Match Play Championship; Paul McGinley wins Scottish Youths' Open Championship at Ladybank and Glenrothes.

1989 Christy O'Connor, Jnr, wins Jersey Open at La Moye; David Feherty wins BMW International Open at Golfplatz, Munich; Ronan Rafferty wins Volvo Masters at Valderrama; Ronan Rafferty wins Scandinavian Enterprise Open at Drottningholms; Stephen Hamill wins Under 25s European Open at Golf du Prièure; Eoghan O'Connell and Garth McGimpsey play on the winning British and Irish team in the Walker Cup at Peachtree, Atlanta ($12\frac{1}{2}$–$11\frac{1}{2}$), the first time the US had been beaten in their own country since the series was instituted in 1922.

Winning trio, Eamonn Darcy, Des Smyth and Ronan Rafferty, pose proudly on the Swilcan Bridge at St Andrews in salute of Ireland's first victory in the Dunhill Nations Cup, 1988.

1990 Eamonn Darcy wins Dubai Desert Classic at Emirates Club, Dubai; Philip Walton wins French Open at Chantilly; Ronan Rafferty wins European Masters at Crans-sur-Serre; Ireland (Ronan Rafferty, David Feherty, Philip Walton) wins Dunhill Nations Cup at St Andrews; Ronan Rafferty wins PLM Open at Bokskogens; Christy O'Connor, Jnr, wins 555 Kenya Open; Ronan Rafferty wins Australian Classic; Darren Clarke wins Spanish Amateur Open Championship; Paul McGinley wins Long Beach Amateur Open, USA.

1991 David Feherty wins Cannes Open at Cannes Mougins; Paul McGinley wins Under 25s European Open at Golf du Prieure; Walker Cup match played for first time ever in Ireland, at Portmarnock (Britain and Ireland 10, USA 14), Ireland represented by Garth McGimpsey, Paul McGinley and Padraig Harrington.

1992 Ronan Rafferty wins Portuguese Open at Vila Sol; Christy O'Connor, Jnr, wins British Masters at Woburn; David Feherty wins Madrid Open at Puerta de Hierro; David Feherty wins South African Bell's Cup; Ronan Rafferty wins Australian Palm Meadows Cup.

1993 Ronan Rafferty wins Hohe Brucke Open at Colony Club, Gutenhof; Darren Clarke wins Belgian Open at Royal Zoute; Des Smyth wins Madrid Open at Puerta de Hierro.

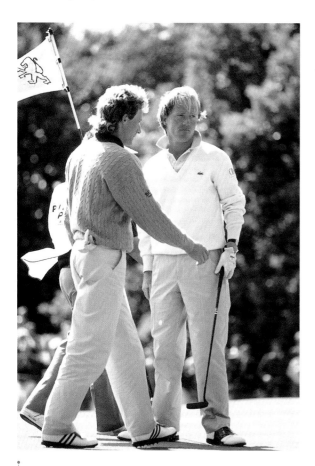

Philip Walton is congratulated by Bernhard Langer after his play-off victory in the 1990 French Open at Chantilly.

Victory at Waterloo for Ireland in the 1983 European Women's Cup, pictured left to right — Philomena Wickham, Mary McKenna, Maureen Madill, Ann Heskin (non playing captain), Richard Bourke (Euro M.P.), Claire Hourihane, Gerry Costello (non playing vice captain), Carol Wickham, Eavan Higgins.

1994 Liam Higgins wins Powell Memorial
Seniors Classic at Collingtree Park;
Liam Higgins wins Seniors Lexus
Trophy, Zurich.

*Jack Nicklaus in action
against Christy
O'Connor, Snr, during
an exhibition match to
mark the official
opening of Mt. Juliet,
July, 1991.*

1995 Philip Walton wins Open Catalonia at
Peralada; Philip Walton wins English
Open at Forest of Arden; Liam Higgins
wins Seniors Lexus Trophy, Zurich;
Jody Fanagan and Padraig Harrington
play key role in Britain and Ireland's
first Walker Cup win since 1971 on
home soil in 14–10 triumph over USA
at Royal Porthcawl, Wales.

1996 Padraig Harrington, in only his fourth
month on his debut European PGA
Tour campaign, wins the Peugeot
Open de Espana at the Club de
Campo, winning a first prize of
£91,666, with a 72 hole total of 272
(16 under par); Paul McGinley shoots a
final round of 62 for a 19 under par
total to win the Austrian Open and
records his first full PGA European

Tour success; Darren Clarke shoots a
final round of 63 to win the German
Masters at Berlin Golf and Country
Club; Valerie Hassett wins the British
Women's Seniors Championship at
Pyle and Kenfig.

Ruggedly beautiful Connemara presents an ideal setting and challenge.

19TH HOLE

JIGS ON THE GREENS

Sunday, 16 October 1988. It was an eerie, chilling sight. St Andrews at 8.30 a.m. was dark and damp. Only the shuffling along the cobblestones of anxious golfers disturbed the quiet of the slumbering university town.

Down at the revered course, the spiritual home of golf, they were swishing the heavy dew from the famous 18th green. The only other movement by the still North Sea was the hunched silhouette of Des Smyth on the practice putting green. Nick Faldo was not far away.

Smyth was finding the timing and tempo for a 54 ft 4½ inch putt, meticulously measured out by his attentive caddy, John O'Reilly. Faldo was practising pitching from 75 yards.

These were the precise shots they were required to play as a result of the Ireland-England Dunhill Cup semi-final being postponed the previous evening. A thick fog had enveloped the links and a tense Faldo, quite correctly, had declined to play on.

On the stroke of the half-hour, play was ordered to recommence. Faldo hit a magnificent shot that landed just seven feet from the hole. It increased the pressure on Smyth, faced with a terrifying putt downhill to a hole that was wickedly cut not much above the incline that falls into the Valley of Sin, that deep ravine that fronts the left-hand side of the spacious green and, since the game began, has endured as sentinel to every transgressor's golfing graveyard.

The eerie sight that greeted Ireland's Des Smyth and England's Nick Faldo on their approach to the famous 18th green at St Andrews in the 1988 Dunhill Nations Cup.

When the fog lifted, a triumphant salute from the winner.

Smyth's light breakfast must have been churning in his nervous stomach. Nevertheless, he defiantly rolled the ball down the sloping green. It ended within three and a half feet of the target, and after Faldo missed with his birdie putt, Smyth holed out for a 69 and a one-shot victory that effectively put Ireland into the final, as Eamonn Darcy was simultaneously sinking a crucial putt on the 17th green to preserve his winning lead over Mark James.

It was a major surprise that Ireland should have reached the final. They had not been given a chance, yet there they were — Smyth, Darcy and Ronan Rafferty — arm in joyous arm trotting back to their hotel for a full Scottish breakfast, pondering their fate in the final against Australia.

They hardly had a team talk in the strict sense, since captain Darcy had set the tone earlier in the week by declaring: 'Now listen to me . . . and then go out and do what you like!' Yet, much as his Irish logic had been the butt of jocose banter, the special atmosphere and spirit that prevailed within the Irish camp contrived to upset the odds as first Canada, then the USA, and now England had all been defeated.

A further measure of the Irish effort was that the opposition had comprised such formidable foes as Dave Barr, Mark McCumber, Curtis Strange, Chip Beck, and even Nick Faldo who had never lost a match in the Dunhill series.

But the Irish were not intimidated by reputations. That was obvious when the line-up for the final was read out: Greg Norman versus Eamonn Darcy, David Graham against Ronan Rafferty, and Rodger Davis versus Des Smyth. Scottish bookmakers sensed they had it right this time: Australia to win!

It did, indeed, seem as if the Irish fairytale was finally coming to an unhappy end as Norman produced the brutal broadside of an incredible 9 under par 63. It was an astonishing opening salvo that certainly left Darcy, who had taken 71, in a bewildered state. It cut no ice with the others.

It is not to take from Rafferty's contribution that in being paired against Graham he got the weakest opponent. Duly, he wrested the initiative from an early stage. Graham erred with a bogey at the 2nd and Rafferty holed from 12 feet for birdie three at the 4th and two putted for another birdie at the long 5th. The template was in place for the Irishman's critical win, by 69 shots to 74.

Still, Des Smyth had gone into his match against Davis under the psychological disadvantage of having been beaten by the Australian in their previous two meetings. When the desperate Irishman was two strokes behind with only three holes remaining, his and Ireland's destiny seemed doomed to defeat.

But from that perilous cliff-top precipice the Irishman was destined to enrich the folklore of St Andrews, and indeed golf itself, by producing the blistering finish of birdie 3, par 4, birdie 3, and turn impending disaster into a champagne celebration.

That memorable sequence was sparked off by a 20 foot putt on the 16th green. The cheer that greeted it must have struck fear and terror into the bones of his Australian opponent. The drive off the 17th tee at St Andrews is notoriously respected in the game as one of the most difficult, given that the ball must be drawn on a right-to-left trajectory back to the fairway over the corner of the imposing Old Course Hotel that stands abreast the infamous Road Hole.

Jigs on the greens at St Andrews from Ronan Rafferty in 1988.

David Feherty after his play-off victory in 1990 and with fellow winning team-mates Ronan Rafferty and Philip Walton.

Smyth duly cracked his shot high and curving on the intended flight path, and as he stood back fulfilled in the knowledge that the appreciation of the crowd's hand-clapping confirmed his success, Davis so badly failed to thread the same needle that his wicked slice waywardly careered into the hotel grounds and ruinously out of bounds.

Smyth had taken control of the match, and when he rolled in another birdie putt on the 18th green there were jigs on the green in salute of Ireland's historic world triumph.

Finally, the younger generation had stepped out of the shadows, their milestone success being good enough to compare with the Canada Cup victory by Christy O'Connor and Harry Bradshaw, thirty years previously.

With the ice broken, further glory was quick to hand. Rafferty was the sole survivor in 1990, teaming up with David Feherty and Philip Walton. A first-day victory over Korea by 3–0 was followed with a 2–1 second-round win over Miguel Angel Jimenez, Jose Maria Canizares and Jose Rivero of Spain. Next, New Zealand's combination of Simon Owen, Frank Nobilo and Greg Turner were swept aside, 2½ to ½, before Ireland once more were inspired to the pinnacle of professional golf team achievement, beating England 3½ to 2½.

This latest chapter in the history of Irish golfing success was marked by the final of the Dunhill Nations Cup being decided in a play-off, with the story further enriched by the way it was done. Feherty, also the captain

Medical student David Sheahan who shocked a field of professional golfers at Royal Dublin in 1962.

of the team, was locked in prolonged battle against Howard Clark. They were into their third extra hole, the 17th! After two good drives, the Englishman played first. He hooked a 3 iron well wide of the green. Feherty was precisely 199 yards from the hole. He, too, chose a 3 iron. He hit it beautifully, softly drawing the ball through the narrow entrance of the tilting green, safely wide of the testing greenside bunker on the left. As if on remotre control, the ball came to rest 15 feet from the hole. Two putts sufficed. Feherty had scaled the heights. Ireland were champions of the world once more!

THE STUDENT PRINCE

On the afternoon of 6 June 1962 a historic golfing feat was achieved when a 22-year-old medical student at University College Dublin, beat a field of top-class professionals in a seventy-two hole strokes tournament at Royal Dublin.

David Sheahan, subsequently to establish a medical practice in Dublin having turned down the choice of going professional, won the Jeyes Pro-Am in a field of forty professionals and forty amateurs. It was a fully fledged seventy-two holes strokes event and was the forerunner to the one-day Pro-Am event which has since become so popular in the game.

A measure of Sheahan's achievement was that he covered the four rounds in 282, 10 under par, with rounds of 69, 72, 72 and 69, leaving the South African, Denis Hutchinson, to take the professional prize and with five Ryder Cup players also in his wake — Christy O'Connor, Bernard Hunt, Dai Rees, Harry Weetman and Ralph Moffatt.

MARCH ON EUROPE

It was at Royal St George's, Sandwich, a venue more associated nowadays as a British Open rota venue, that Ireland made amateur golfing history on a chilly Sunday evening in June 1965.

For the first time Ireland had entered the European Amateur Cup and faced England in the deciding match, with everything depending on the outcome of Tom Craddock against Martin Christmas.

An eerie silence and the weight of Europe hung over the Irishman, who needed to get down from 35 yards short of the 18th green in a chip and putt to secure overall victory. 'The greatest shot of my career' was how the defiant Irishman later described an inch-perfect stroke of surgeon-like delicacy as he 'glued' the ball against the flagstick.

Even though England won the match 6–3, it was Ireland's title on the basis of

cumulative matches won throughout the championship.

Craddock, Joe Carr, Vincent Nevin, David Sheahan (Michael Craigan, Bill McCrea and Rupert Staunton were the other team members) were also present when Ireland defended the title in Italy two years later in as dramatic a manner. The tension of the famous occasion in the Circolo Golf Club at Turin was ultimately released as the jubilant team members tossed their non-playing captain, Cecil Ewing, fully clothed into the swimming pool!

The four survivors from Sandwich were joined by Tom Egan and Peter Flaherty, and it was Egan, a jeweller from Cork, who was the match-winning hero. Despite feeling ill and having to get on-course attention from Dr Billy O'Sullivan, Egan's short and accurate play was entirely suited to the heavily tree-lined course and he always had the measure

History makers in Italy. The Ireland team which won the European Amateur Championship in 1967. From left to right: Tom O'Donnell, President, Golfing Union of Ireland; Vincent Nevin; Peter Flaherty; David Sheahan; Cecil Ewing, non-playing captain; Joe Carr; Tom Egan, Tom Craddock; Bill Menton, General Secretary, GUI.

of Roger Legarde, the leading member of the French team.

The Corkman came to the 18th with a hole up advantage, and while Legarde gave himself a chance by hitting his second shot to within 10 feet of the hole, with Egan short on the apron, it was to be Ireland's glory as Egan rolled his effort so close to the target that the putt for par was conceded and Ireland were winners when Legard just failed to force a play-off. Ireland had also earned the distinction of recording their first ever team victory in continental Europe.

It was not until 1983, at the Golf de Chantilly Club, twenty miles from Paris, that Ireland won again. The Carr tradition lived on as Joe's son, John, played a key role in a team also comprising Philip Walton, Garth McGimpsey, Arthur Pierse, Mick Morris and Tom Cleary. The coaching policy adopted by the Golfing Union of Ireland was beginning to bear fruit and the combination of John Garner's teaching and the astuteness of Brendan Edwards as non-playing captain succeeded brilliantly.

First-day victory over France by 6–1 and the second-day elimination of Scotland by 4–3, set up a final showdown against a Spanish side led by Jose Maria Olazabal. Interestingly, the Spanish captain moved Olazabal from the No. 1 singles in order to avoid a clash with Walton! The fear in the

Spanish camp was duly endorsed as they went down by 5–2. Triumphant Ireland shook to the roots the austere Chantilly club with their mood of celebration. The local district band, huddled behind the clubhouse, frantically raced against the clock to learn the Irish national anthem from a tape that had been hurriedly dispatched from the embassy in Paris.

Four years later, Ireland were crowned champions again, in Murhof, Austria, coincidentally on the same day that Ireland were winning the European Ladies' Championship in Brussels.

The Austrian victory may stand out as the best of four Euro titles won when the 90 degree heat is taken into account and the fact that Ireland beat England in the final. In five previous European battles against the English, Ireland had won only once, at the semi-final stages in Turin, so it became a special occasion on beating England this time $4\frac{1}{2}$ to $2\frac{1}{2}$.

Such was the wholly conscientious, if slightly bizarre, approach of Eamon Curran as non-playing captain that he wrote a letter to the headmistress of the local school, seeking the release of two young girls he wanted to employ as caddies. He had seen these girls, who turned out to be the Austrian girls and junior champions, playing the course; so when he persuaded a bemused schoolmistress to grant permission for their release, Garth McGimpsey and Eoghan O'Connell had the services of the two best caddies available.

Neil Anderson, John McHenry, Liam MacNamara and Padraig Hogan were also in devastating form. They shielded themselves from the scorching sunshine with umbrellas, first beating West Germany, then France, and finally England.

European Cup.

OLYMPIC GOLD

Until the achievement of Michelle Smith winning three gold and one bronze medal at the 1996 Atlanta Olympic Games, the greatest occasion in the history of Irish teams competing in Olympic Games was at Los Angeles in 1932. Surprisingly it had a golf connection!

Within the space of just ten minutes, Ireland won two gold medals when Bob Tisdall won the 400 metres hurdles and was followed by Dr Pat O'Callaghan's success in the hammer. An acknowledged contributing factor in their achievement was the part played by Ballybunion Golf Club.

Prior to their departure to the games, the Irish track and field team of four, also including Michael Murphy in the steeplechase and Eamonn Fitzgerald who finished fourth in the hop, step and jump, had spent a fortnight preparing on the golf course. Tisdall had hurdles erected on the 18th fairway (now the 5th) and did all his practice there, claiming that the springiness of the turf added substantially to his speed, while O'Callaghan believed that Ballybunion Golf Club 'was the ideal spot, calm and peaceful'.

A RARE PHENOMENON

Beware the phenomenon of Killsaheen! Among the rarest sights through the haze of the shimmering Atlantic is the phenomenon of Killsaheen, or Killsthaheen, as it is sometimes called. It takes the form of a spectacle which, on a rare calm day, appears in the sea off the clifftop coastline of

THE IRISH PRE[SS]

FRIDAY, JANUARY 15, 1988

The Truth in the News

Golf buff buried at Ballybunion course

An American golfing fanatic thought so much of Ballybunion golf course that he ordered his body to be flown from Los Angeles for burial beside the famous international course.

And on new Year's Eve, the remains of 43-year-old Martin McDermott were interred at Killakenny Cemetery, close to the first tee at Ballybunion.

Mr. Sean Walsh, secretary of Ballybunion golf course, said yesterday that the first most of the local golfers knew of the interment was "when it was all over. But I really was not all that surprised; it is the kind of thing the Americans might do. They hold this course in very high esteem and come back year after year to play it. This man came back for good."

The dead man had played Ballybunion only twice, in 1984 and 1986, but was so taken with the place that he wished to be buried close by, according to his wife, Vickki, who had the body flown the 6,000 miles across the Atlantic.

"It was the one wish he had left," she said after the burial at which local parish priest, Fr. Michael Galvin, officiated.

*Ballybunion, and the
vision of Killsaheen.*

the Ballybunion links, near the long Clare
Peninsula, not far from Loop Head. The
peninsula forms the western arm enclosing
the mouth of the River Shannon.

Local people who have witnessed this
amazing vision say it consists of a large arch,
or bridge, with people walking about, as if at
a fair, while in one place close to the arch
can be seen an old woman sitting by a cart or
table. The beshawled lady is evidently selling
her wares to those passing by.

This extraordinary sight traditionally lasts
from ten to fifteen minutes before,
mysteriously, it fades away, leaving the sea
clear and blank as it was before.

Beware! While it is a unique privilege to
see this vision, it is not altogether a welcome
one, as tradition holds that those who
witness the phenomenon will die within
seven years!

However, you may relax! There is no need
for undue alarm, as there are a few people

who have had the privilege and are still hale and hearty many times seven years after their experience.

What causes this Ballybunion golf links phenomenon?

The shape and general appearance of the arch suggests that it is a mirage, reflecting the silhouette of the Spanish Arch in Galway city, which is situated due north of Ballybunion and which may be reflected in the sky in certain conditions of the light and cloud formation over the sea.

LONG DROP CLUB

The members of a Ryder Cup team, including Christy O'Connor and Norman Drew, clearly remember the date 29 October 1959. Every year on that date a ritual is maintained by all the members of the team who drink a toast in remembrance of a terrifying experience. It was the occasion of the Long Drop.

The flight from Los Angeles to Palm Springs in a twin-engine propeller aircraft, transporting the British and Irish team to the thirteenth Ryder Cup match at the Eldorado Country Club, ran into a raging thunderstorm and nearly plunged out of the sky. When the troubled flight, which at one stage plummeted from 13,000 feet down to 6,000, finally had to turn back to Los Angeles, shaken passengers were relieved to have survived and voted unanimously to continue their

journey by Greyhound coach rather than by air.

En route they founded the J-L Long Drop Club, the J-L standing for Jolly Lucky. They had cards printed with the inscription:

J-L Long Drop Club
5.30 p.m. October 29th, 1959
Los Angeles to Palm Springs
ALMOST!

It was the only Ryder Cup match in which Norman Drew played. It was the third of ten for Christy O'Connor. The only other Irishman involved in the scary incident was Barry Nolan, golf correspondent for Independent Newspapers.

The other British and Irish team members were: Dai Rees, Peter Alliss, Eric Brown, Ken Bousfield, Bernard Hunt, Peter Mills, Dave Thomas and Harry Weetman.

*Historic Rosapenna
— 18th hole, Par 4.*

Golf as Gaeilge, at the Irish-named Ceann Sibeal Golf Club on the Dingle Peninsula.

115

PROUD RECORD

In the history of the Walker Cup, instituted in 1927, Britain and Ireland has beaten the USA only four times. On each occasion there has been a substantial Irish contribution.

Coincidentally, the first two victories were achieved at St Andrews, with Jimmy Bruen and Cecil Ewing on the historic 1938 side, first-time winners by $7\frac{1}{2}$–$4\frac{1}{2}$.

Walker Cup hero Jody Fanagan is congratulated by British and Irish captain Clive Brown and fellow team members after he clinched victory for the home team at Royal Porthcawl in 1995.

Considering that it took thirty-three further years of golfing gloom to repeat that victory, there was great celebration at the Home of Golf in 1971 when Roddy Carr made such an invaluable contribution to a 13–11 win.

With his father, Joe, who was ten times a Walker Cup player, young Roddy, then just 21 years of age, entered history as the only father and son to be so honoured. And how he marked the occasion, being undefeated in his four matches and beating Jim Simons on the 18th hole of the final day!

As an indication of just how difficult it has been to beat the American amateurs, there was a further gap of eighteen years to Britain and Ireland's next triumph, achieved with the notable help of Garth McGimpsey and Eoghan O'Connell at the Peachtree Club in Atlanta.

The occasion stands out as the first time the Americans, featuring Phil Mickelson, Robert Gamez and Jay Sigel, were beaten ($11\frac{1}{2}$–$12\frac{1}{2}$) in their own country. It was of particular significance for Ireland. If Phil Mickelson was giving a first glimpse on the international stage of his prowess with a 4 and 2 first-day win over McGimpsey, the scales were balanced in the breathless finish of the concluding singles next day when O'Connell reached the peak of his great amateur career by holding the top American team player to a half.

Emerging undefeated from one of the most nerve-racking matches in the series, O'Connell was perilously one down to Mickelson with only two to play, but defiantly won the 17th and was held to a half only when the lanky American left-hander holed from nine feet on the final green.

In 1995 at Royal Porthcawl, the US were cock-a-hoop with a side led by the great Tiger Woods. Once more, however, Ireland was seen to play a critical role in a shock result. Padraig Harrington, three wins from four matches in a memorable amateur swan-song, and debutant Jody Fanagan, with three wins from three, the only unbeaten player on either side, provided much of the inspiration. In point of fact, in a 14–10 win, it was Fanagan and his 3 and 2 win over Jerry Courville that sealed victory.

IRELAND'S FULL LIST OF WALKER CUP CAPPED PLAYERS IS:

Joe Carr (1947, 1949, 1951, 1953, 1955, 1957, 1959, 1961, 1963, (1965, non-playing Captain), 1967); Roddy Carr (1971); Tom Craddock (1967, 1969); John Burke (1932); Jimmy Bruen (1938, 1949, 1951); Raymond Burns (1993); Norman Drew (1953); Cecil Ewing (1936, 1938, 1947, 1949, 1951, 1955); Jody Fanagan (1995); Padraig Harrington (1991, 1993); Charles Hezlet (1924, 1926, 1928); David Madeley (1963); Pat Mulcare (1975); Max McCready (1949, 1951); Garth McGimpsey (1985, 1989, 1991); Paul McGinley (1991); John McHenry (1987); Noel C. Martin (1928); Eoghan O'Connell (1989); Arthur Pierse (1983); Ronan Rafferty (1981); Philip Walton (1981, 1983).

HACKETT'S LEGACY

While much of the natural landscape of Ireland is particularly suitable for golf, the skill of many outstanding international golf architects has enhanced nature's gifts. However, one of the greatest of these is himself an Irishman.

Eddie Hackett's more notable designs are the widely acclaimed Waterville links in Kerry, the Murvagh course in Donegal, Enniscrone in County Sligo, Malahide's new twenty-seven holes complex near Dublin, Connemara in County Galway and the Killeen course in Killarney. Appropriately, he was also the one chosen to extend the course at historic Rosapenna in north-west Donegal, where the original designers were none other than Old Tom Morris and, later, Harry Vardon.

Born in 1910, Hackett only discovered a penchant for design by accident. He had become the first established amateur to turn professional in Ireland, making the transition in 1932, and his varied career saw him work with his great friend, Henry Cotton, at the Belgian Club, Waterloo; in Johannesburg; at Elm Park in south Dublin; and then, as successor to the famous Willie Nolan, at Portmarnock, where he was in residence from 1939 to 1950, before handing over to Harry Bradshaw.

Dogged by ill health all his life — he had a kidney removed in 1936 and was in hospital for almost a year when he had meningitis in 1954 — Hackett's playing career was greatly affected as a result. However, anything he lost out on as a player, he more than gained in the reputation he built as an above average club professional and teacher.

As a player, he did compete in the British Open and one of his most cherished memories was having lunch with James Braid, Harry Vardon and J. H. Taylor. He quite literally bumped into these golfing greats in the Royal Liverpool clubhouse during the 1936 championship as he searched for a vacant seat in the dining room!

The late Eddie Hackett, Ireland's most prolific golf course designer.

When the Golfing Union of Ireland looked for a professional to tour the country teaching in the early 1960s, Hackett was given the job by the then honorary secretary, Bill Menton, and it was the latter's astuteness that also steered Hackett towards golf course improvement and design when the governing body was inundated with enquiries during the golfing boom of the 1960s.

In addition to the well-known courses to which Hackett has contributed, he believes there are upwards of eighty others he has designed or remodelled. There is hardly a county in which he has not left his mark — superb work carried out for an incredibly modest financial return.

'I find that nature is the best architect. I just try to dress up what the good Lord has already provided,' he said on his 86th birthday, shortly before his death in 1997.

A CHRISTMAS REMINDER

A Christmas card pops through the letter-box of Christy O'Connor, Jnr's, home in County Galway. It contains more than the sentiments of the season. It encapsulates all that is best in golf.

'You did yourself and your country proud — good luck to you,' is the heartfelt message from Fred Couples, the unwitting American at the wrong end of an incredible incident that decided the destination of a Ryder Cup.

It was late in the afternoon of Sunday, 24 September 1989, when anxious Tony Jacklin, the European team captain, coaxed 'just one more swing for Ireland' from Christy O'Connor, then in the centre of the 18th fairway at the Belfry and at the heart of one of the most famous moments in sport.

The response from the Irishman was the dramatic two iron shot that covered an astonishing 229 yards distance and landed within three feet of the hole.

*Magic moments in the Ryder Cup, provided by
Christy O'Connor, Jnr, at The Belfry in 1989. . .*

. . . by Eamonn Darcy at Muirfield Village in 1987 . . .

. . . and by Philip Walton at Oak Hill in 1995.

It was quite an astounding performance, considering the pressure and the life and death scenario of so many other matches on the water-festooned 18th hole on the same day. It so flummoxed poor old Fred Couples that he just could not reply. His feeble 9 iron was wide of the green, and when he could not salvage a chip and putt, he had no option but to concede to the Irishman.

Victory for O'Connor effectively secured a tied match for Europe and the retention of the Ryder Cup. With Ronan Rafferty also marking this historic day with a win over the reigning British Open champion, Mark Calcavecchia, there was double-celebration for the Irish as they had made such a rich contribution to one of the greatest golf matches ever played.

While O'Connor, Jnr, provided his sensational touch with his approach over the lake to the final green, it was the drive of a lifetime that set it up for Rafferty, in that he was not required to hit his ball again.

What is forever etched in the mind is the precocious manner in which the Irishman met the challenge of the fearsome drive over the lake off the tee at the 18th where Calcavecchia, like so many other Americans to be found wanting on the day, not alone met a watery grave with his drive, but thereafter well and truly drowned his chances and that of America by hitting his following shot into the next stretch of water to be negotiated. Game, set and match to Rafferty.

It seemed entirely appropriate that Ireland's reputation in the world pecking order of golf should have been so enhanced in this grand manner. But then 1989 confirmed the fact that Irish professional golf had arrived at its highest point in modern times.

Remember how, when the 1987 Ryder Cup was so precariously balanced on a knife edge at Muirfield Village, it was Eamonn Darcy who saved the day. This was the occasion when Europe defied all the odds by becoming the first team ever to beat the Americans in their own backyard in the sixty year history of the Ryder Cup series. The margin was 15–13.

The match was played on the Muirfield Village course in deference to Jack Nicklaus, born just up the highway in Columbus, Ohio. Ironically, it became his graveyard during three incredible days in autumn, as the shift in the balance of world golfing power truly turned in favour of Europe.

There was Torrance and Langer and Faldo and Woosnam and Ballesteros and Olazabal. And there was Darcy.

On the day of the fateful match-deciding singles, an illustration of the closeness of the battle was that eight matches went down to the last hole. The Americans won none of them, most significantly when Darcy, who had been one down with two to play against Ben Crenshaw, squared his match at the 17th and then came out of a greenside bunker at the last and holed a five foot putt. It had a wickedly deceptive left to right swing. It was downhill — on a lightning fast green. The difficulty begs no further qualification.

Nicklaus acknowledged the Irishman's achievement: 'I would put Darcy's putt as the final nail in our coffin. He holed it like a man and the memory should live with him forever!'

As much by ability as by joyous coincidence, Philip Walton became the next Irishman to effectively seal a winning Ryder Cup effort for Europe when he provided the critical point at the Oak Hill Country Club,

Rochester, New York, in 1995. The visiting team's hopes seemed distant when they went into the deciding twelve singles trailing by 7–9 and, furthermore, when Seve Ballesteros lost the No. 1 singles to Tom Lehman.

It was something of a sensation, therefore, that America should crumble from that seemingly invincible position; but if Nick Faldo's recovery against a faltering Curtis Strange served as the catalyst, it was down to Walton and the dogged way he held out to beat Jay Haas in the very last match alive.

The Irishman chipped from the edge of the final green to 15 feet and then, with the weight of the golfing world upon his shoulders, he putted the ball to the edge of the hole. Europe were winners by a point!

Once more, European golf was seen to be safe in the hands of an Irishman.

RYDER CUP TANTRUMS

'A classic — with a vexed needle', was how the media headlines proclaimed a battle at the heart of Britain and Ireland's victory over America in the 1957 incident-packed Ryder Cup match at Lindrick. The reference was to the momentous clash involving Ireland's Christy O'Connor and Dow Finsterwald, a bad-tempered American.

O'Connor and Harry Bradshaw became the first Irishmen to play on a winning Ryder Cup team (7½–4½), but the occasion is also remembered for the fact that Finsterwald refused to shake O'Connor's hand after the match.

While Bradshaw was playing out a half with the US Open champion, Dick Mayer, O'Connor, 32-years-old at the time, was locked in a fractious affair with 27-year-old Finsterwald, who had come to Britain

nominated as the best young prospect of the time on the US Tour.

The Americans had travelled so confidently that they insured the Ryder Cup trophy for a further two years — before they had even left America! They had a star line-up, comprising Art Wall, Doug Ford, Ted Kroll, Tommy Bolt, Dick Mayer, Ed Furgol, Lionel Hebert and Dow Finsterwald.

The British and Irish team was Harry Bradshaw, Peter Mills, Peter Alliss, Bernard Hunt, Harry Weetman, Max Faulkner, Eric Brown, Dai Rees (the captain), Ken Bousfield and Christy O'Connor.

It was billed as another lop-sided encounter: the Americans were said to be the most stylish side since the war. Although there was no Hogan, Snead, Demaret or Middlecoff, it was suggested that the Americans had such good technical swing quality that they gave the impression that the golden age of the 1920s had returned for the USA.

All seemed to be going according to plan when the Americans led by 3–1 heading into the eight singles. More so since the home team were at loggerheads, disgruntled that their wives and sweethearts were not permitted to share the same hotel, and up in arms that Weetman had been left out of the singles.

Quite sensationally, Britain and Ireland turned it about in the singles. O'Connor showed fine inspiration, winning on the 12th green, albeit against the backdrop of one of the most vexed Ryder Cup matches ever played.

Each threw the rule-book at the other, O'Connor being given the 3rd hole when a shaken Finsterwald stretched out in anger and hooked the ball back as it was still in motion after he had missed a short putt; and

Finsterwald claiming the 9th hole in the afternoon of the scheduled thirty-six hole match when O'Connor assumed that a putt of just one inch would be conceded for a half and proceeded to pick up the ball and head for the next tee.

In the event, O'Connor won the match in a canter by 7 and 6, but Finsterwald would not shake hands and he also declined much later when members of both teams attempted to pour cold water on the fiery talking point that became part of Ryder Cup history.

FRED DALY'S SHRINE

In a corner of the lounge at the Balmoral Golf Club on the outskirts of Belfast, there is a monument to the club's most famous member, Fred Daly.

The Fred Daly Corner, as it is respectfully referred to, is a section of the clubhouse festooned with memorabilia associated with a man who holds the distinction of being Ireland's only British Open winner. A multitude of items associated with Daly's great and many golfing achievements are on permanent view, and each year hundreds of visitors call by, as if on pilgrimage. It is a permanent reminder of the growing interest in the history of golf, all its old historic milestones, its old clubs, balls, books and trophies. It is also a lasting tribute to a great man.

World War II deprived Daly of much golfing opportunity, but as soon as peace was restored and tournament golf resumed, he began to make his mark.

The highlight, of course, was his British Open victory at Hoylake in 1947, an Everest that encapsulated all that was best in his game. After confident opening rounds of 73 and 70 in good weather conditions, featuring some canny play with his famous 2X iron, he slumped to a 78 in the third round on the morning of the final day. When the little Irishman then began the final round in the afternoon by taking 38 to the turn, all seemed lost, until he dug deep to summon his tenacious fighting spirit and carve out an incredible win.

The turning point was evidenced when holes 10 to 14 were covered in just 17 shots, an amazing two over threes! At the core of the rally was the defiant manner in which he demonstrated once more his ability to hole vital putts when under extreme pressure. For example, he holed a putt from twenty yards at the 13th. Then at the 18th he got down from 12 yards for a birdie 3, and as the weather broke thereafter, Daly was ensconced in the shelter of the clubhouse as the rest unavailingly tried to catch him.

A measure of his merit was that the following year he was second, then third in 1950, and in 1952 he was third again. A first, a second and twice third in the British Open is an unmatched record among Irish professionals.

Fred Daly is well deserving of his shrine.

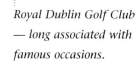

Royal Dublin Golf Club — long associated with famous occasions.

STRANGE HAPPENINGS

In the final round of the 1972 Penfold PGA Tournament at Queen's Park, Bournemouth, when Christy O'Connor, Snr, arrived at the 6th hole, he was unable to find his ball. The spectators were asked to look in their clothing and a man found the ball in his pocket.

◆ ◆ ◆

At Midleton, County Cork, in 1922, a member of the club, Mr McEvoy, drove from the 3rd tee, the ball entering the ear of a donkey. After a delay the donkey tossed its head and the ball fell out.

◆ ◆ ◆

At Royal Dublin in July 1936, in the Irish Open Championship, Bobby Locke played his tee shot at the 12th hole, but the ball could not be found on arrival at the green. The pin was removed and it was discovered that the ball was entangled in the flag. It dropped near the edge of the hole and Locke sank the putt for a birdie 2.

◆ ◆ ◆

In 1936, at the Bellevue Zoo, Belfast, a fatality occurred when a Himalayan bear died from swallowing a golf ball. The bear, which was a favourite with visitors, sat up and begged, and some irresponsible person threw it a golf ball.

◆ ◆ ◆

Playing over the Killarney course in June 1957, a golfer sliced his ball into one of the lakes and knocked out a trout rising to catch a fly. His partner waded into the water to get the ball — and the trout.

◆ ◆ ◆

Deliberate interference by spectators with balls in play during important money matches was not unknown in the old days. Tom Morris refused to play Willie Park at Musselburgh because of interference by the spectators. In another challenge arranged for the same course in 1895, the barracking of the crowd and interference with play was so bad that for the Park–Harry Vardon challenge, Vardon refused to accept Musselburgh as the venue.

Even in modern times spectators have been known to interfere deliberately with play balls, though it is usually children. In the 1972 Penfold Tournament at Queen's Park, Bournemouth, Christy O'Connor, Jnr, had his ball stolen by a young boy but, not being told of this at the time, he had to take the penalty for a lost ball. O'Connor finished in a tie for first place with Peter Oosterhuis, but lost the play-off.

ACES HIGH

Since the day of the first known hole in one by Tom Morris, Jnr, at the 145 yard 8th hole at Prestwick in the 1868 British Open Championship, holes in one, even in championships, have become too numerous for each to be recorded. Only where other unusual or interesting circumstances prevail are the instances shown here:

◆ ◆ ◆

1933: In the final of the Irish Amateur Open Championship over 36 holes at Newcastle, County Down, Eric Fiddian (Stourbridge) met Jack McLean. In the morning, Fiddian made the 128 yard 7th hole in one stroke and in the afternoon he did the 14th hole of 205 yards also in one. However, these remarkable scores did not carry him to victory as he lost by 3 and 2.

◆ ◆ ◆

Two holes in one and still beaten - unlucky Eric Fiddian.

1953: In the first round of the £3,000 Irish Open at Belvoir Park, Belfast, Eric Brown holed his tee shot at the 196 yards 16th hole. It helped him to break the course record with 66 (34–32).

◆ ◆ ◆

1974: In the Home Amateur Internationals at Harlech, Wales, Sandy Pirie of Scotland holed in one at the last hole to win against Ireland's Pat Mulcare and Raymond Kane.

◆ ◆ ◆

1975: In the last round of the Carroll's Irish Open at Woodbrook, Christy O'Connor, Snr, holed in one at the 17th hole, to be followed ninety minutes later by John McTear doing exactly the same. They shared the special £1,000 prize and O'Connor used the champagne to toast victory to his nephew, Christy, Jnr.

◆ ◆ ◆

1988: Mary Anderson, a biochemistry student at Trinity College, Dublin, holed in one at the 290 yards 6th hole at The Island Club, near Dublin.

◆ ◆ ◆

1996: Paul McGinley scored a hole in one at the 9th hole on his way to a second round 65 in the British Open Championship at Royal Lytham and St Anne's.

LONG DISTANCE

Tommie Campbell featured in the *Guinness Book of Records* as hitting the longest drive, without any favourable conditions prevailing, with a drive of 392 yards at the Dun Laoghaire Club in July 1964.

During the Irish Professional Championship at Waterville in 1986, four noted long hitting players tried for the longest carry record over water, across a lake in the grounds of a local hotel. Liam Higgins, the local professional, carried 310 yards, and Paul Leonard 311, beating the previous record by two yards.

Where an outside agency has assisted the length of a shot, Liam Higgins hit a drive of 632 yards down the runway at Baldonnel, the Irish Air Corps base, in 1986.

◆ ◆ ◆

At the Home International matches at Portmarnock in 1949, a driving competition was held in which all the players in the English, Welsh, Scottish and Irish teams competed. The actual carry was measured and the longest was 280 yards by Jimmy Bruen.

◆ ◆ ◆

A £1 million prize for a hole in one! That was the startling prize put on offer as an attraction during the three week national festival, called An Tostal, in 1953. The unusual twist was that the competition took the format of a cross-country test in which 150 golfers drove from the first tee at Cill Dara Golf Club and holed out eventually on the 18th green, five miles away on the Curragh.

The hazards to be negotiated included the main Dublin-Cork railway line and road, the Curragh racecourse, Irish army tank ranges and about 150 telephone lines.

The Golden Ball Trophy was for the best gross and it went to the renowned long hitter and player, Joe Carr, with the remarkably good score of 52 shots.

TRIPLE CROWNS

Champagne flowed in suitable celebration of golfing history at Lahinch on Friday, 11 September 1987: Ireland won the Triple Crown for the first time in the Men's Amateur Home International Championship.

Lahinch milestone: The Ireland team which made history by winning the Triple Crown for the first time, at Lahinch in 1987. Back row, left to right: Garth McGimpsey, Paul Rayfus, Liam MacNamara, Gerry O'Brien (President, Golfing Union of Ireland), Neil Anderson, Darren Clarke, Padraig Hogan; front row, left to right: Denis O'Sullivan, Arthur Pierse, Eddie Power, Eamon Curran (non-playing captain), Barry Reddan, Mark Gannon.

This annual event between Ireland, England, Scotland and Wales was instituted in 1932, but in the forty-six championships held in the intervening years, Ireland had never managed to beat the three other nations at one championship.

At last, the historic Grand Slam was achieved with a final day $10\frac{1}{2}$–$4\frac{1}{2}$ win over Scotland, following a 6–4 win over England, when the first day's play was curtailed to singles because of bad weather, and an 8–7 success over Wales.

The celebration and emotion surrounding Ireland's unprecedented effort was all the greater at this famous golfing venue as this was the climax of a season in which the European Cup had been won in Austria in June.

'Now I can retire happy,' said non-playing captain Eamon Curran, whose three year term had seen him become Ireland's most successful captain ever. It was a fitting tribute to a man whose conscientious dedication and astute handling of his players had been a feature of that momentous time in Irish golf.

The history-making winning Triple Crown Irish team on the final day was: Neil Anderson, Eddie Power, Garth McGimpsey, Liam MacNamara, Mark Gannon, Barry Reddan, Padraig Hogan, Dennis O'Sullivan, Arthur Pierse and Paul Rayfus.

Darren Clarke, a 19-year-old new cap, was chosen only for the opening singles against England.

As if inspired by that breakthrough, a second Triple Crown was achieved at Conway in Wales three years later. This time George Crosbie was at the helm and the man who had been on many teams in the past as a player, this time achieved his ultimate fulfilment as a Triple Crown winning captain.

Considering that Darren Clarke and Jim Carvill had just turned professional, there was no sense of optimism as the Irish hopefuls headed to the north Wales coast, with England, looking for a third successive title, declared outright favourites. However, Irish hearts and spirits were raised with wins by 9–6 and 11–4 over Scotland and Wales on the first two days.

A major contribution was an undefeated debut by 19-year-old Padraig Harrington. He then made it five wins from five when the foursomes were tied against England, and when he went back out in the sunshine and was 4 under par when completing his own grand slam with victory over the English champion, Ian Garbutt, on the 18th green, the rest of his colleagues responded and a fine 8–7 win was achieved.

The survivors from Lahinch were: Liam MacNamara, Mark Gannon, Neil Anderson and Garth McGimpsey, and they were augmented by Harrington, Jody Fanagan, Paul McGinley, David Errity, Niall Goulding, Ken Kearney and Gary MacNeill.

Beautiful Galway Bay, another west coast jewel.

The Blackwood Golf Centre in Bangor, County Down: a pay-and-play concept of great popularity.

IRELAND'S NEW GOLFING GEMS

ONE OF THE MOST AMAZING DEVELOPMENTS OF MODERN IRISH GOLF has been the phenomenal increase in the number of courses. Such has been the rate in growth that Ireland has now exceeded the recommended ideal ratio of golf courses per head of population! There are now in excess of 350 clubs affiliated to the Golfing Union of Ireland, with more than 100 established since 1983.

In its comprehensive paper, 'The Demand For Golf', published in 1988, the Royal and Ancient concluded that the right balance in Britain and Northern Ireland was one club per 15,000 head of population. The ratio in Ireland is now 1:14,000.

It is little wonder that Ireland is perceived as a land of golf, thriving in the wake of what can only be described as a sporting gold-rush!

The dividends are manifold: most notably by way of providing facilities for the vast numbers wanting to play and, in tandem, by developing a market which has contributed handsomely to the economy by way of employment and tourism revenue.

Just as the boom witnessed in the growth of the game in the late 1950s and early 1960s found its roots in the tournament achievements of stalwarts like Harry Bradshaw and Christy O'Connor, the advent of televised international golf and the creation of folk heroes Arnold Palmer, Jack Nicklaus and Gary Player, the resurgence from the mid-1980s can also be traced to some critical developments.

One of the most significant developments was the flight by farmers and landowners from farmland, encouraged by restrictive European Union quotas. At the same time, the trend was helped by inducements from Bord Fáilte (the Irish Tourist Board) by way of development grants from European Union funding.

An example of the growth rate and expenditure in Irish golf is that well in excess of £200 million has been invested in new golfing properties. Privately owned facilities account for much of this spending, with the consequence that it is believed that up to

The quite magnificent European Club, amid the dunes at Brittas Bay.

half of Ireland's golfers will be playing over commercial and privately owned properties early into the next century.

All the while, the numbers of those playing the game has increased significantly. There are now approximately 200,000 male players affiliated to the Golfing Union of Ireland. The percentage increase among women players is at least comparable, as the official figure heads towards 50,000.

It remains to be seen if the supply of courses outstrips demand. In the clamour to capitalise on the 'golf rush', some errors of judgment may yet be seen to have been

made. Only those who have chosen their locations wisely and who are commercially driven will survive in the long term. It is essential, therefore, that proper marketing is to the fore which, of course, would indicate that pricing, in terms of annual subscriptions and day-to-day green fees, will be kept competitively in favour of the player!

Already, one of the virtues shining through the boom is that in Ireland you can still enjoy the experience of a round of golf on a perfectly good course for between £10 and £20 ($16 and $32).

The captivating Druid's Glen encompassing the 174 yards, par 3 12th hole, within which lies the preserved stone holy table of pre-Christian worship on a hillside overlooking the green.

The changing face of Irish golf is classically illustrated in the creation by Jack Nicklaus of the magnificent course at Mount Juliet as depicted in the 3rd and 14th holes (left) and also in the spectacular 7th hole at the Arnold Palmer designed K club.

Golfers can arrive by car or by cruiser on the Shannon River to a private jetty that is a feature of the new Glasson Golf and Country Club at Athlone in County Westmeath.

Opened in 1993, the decision by landowner Tom Reid to quit farming and convert his prime property to golfing use was a wise one because the Glasson course in the heart of the Irish midlands is being widely acclaimed as one of the modern period's best products.

Designed by Christy O'Connor, Jnr, the Glasson course of 7,120 yards is a tough one. However, its magical setting overlooking Lough Ree, one of the Shannon's largest lakes, is one of the most scenic anywhere in Irish golf.

The 14th par 5, starting from amid the woods and tumbling down to the lake shore, followed by the par 3 15th to an island green, may become one of the most photographed holes in Ireland.

Another major factor in the growth of golf is the fact that Nicklaus and Palmer, instrumental in the first instance in creating a new awareness of the game, were brought in to design courses, which further fired the imagination of those wanting to capitalise on a worldwide market growth.

Changing practices in the workplace, a greater emphasis on leisure time activity and, of course, the two well-publicised, world status wins by Ireland in the Dunhill Nations Cup at St Andrews in the 1980s, together with the trail being blazed also in successive Ryder Cup triumphs and in tournaments generally by a successful new breed of Irish professionals, all combined to increase the demand.

Encompassed in much of the present day contribution to Ireland's rich and rare architectural culture are elements that may well be foreign to the connoisseur. Cascading waterfalls; white, shimmering sand in irregularly shaped bunkers; the remorseless vision and challenge of water; high, multi-tiered greens; extravagant earth moving and landscaping: these are components not synonymous with the traditional golfing face of Ireland. However, each of these elements has its own place in modern golfing society and together they serve to keep Ireland in the shop window of the game.

It can be said that the changing face of Irish golf represents the updating to modern architectural standards of a product which retains its special Irish flavour.

Mount Juliet at Thomastown, County Kilkenny, and the K Club at Straffan, County Kildare, underline that virtue. They are the inspirational work of successful businessmen who want to give Ireland a standard of golf not previously available.

'Building a golf course is my total expression. My golf game can only go on so long. But what I have learned can be put into a piece of ground to last beyond me.' This is the Jack Nicklaus philosophy at the heart of the greatly acclaimed Mount Juliet, which is most frequently voted Ireland's best parkland course.

It is Ireland's first purpose-built golf course in the category of 'stadium golf', in so far as it is the first ever architectural effort in Ireland partly constructed with the spectator in mind. That was one of the many virtues to have shone through during the several stagings of Irish Open Championships.

Glasson Golf and Country Club, backing on to the River Shannon.

Adare Manor is laid on lush County Limerick countryside with an historic castle hotel as an imposing backdrop.

When Nick Faldo visited Ballyliffen *en route* to playing in the Irish Open Championship in 1993, he stirred an interest in history and created an awareness of one of Ireland's finest golfing resorts.

Amid the spectacular dunes and scenery of the Inishowen Peninsula, Ireland's most northerly club is in an area steeped in the very best golfing traditions.

Ballyliffen, Buncrana, Portsalon, Rosapenna, Dunfanaghy, North West, Nairn and Portnoo: every one a golfing gem, whose collective case can rival the more lauded south-west pocket of the country in terms of tradition and beauty.

While golfing throughout Donegal you will experience a string of great places to play on the best of links terrain and where the game has been played since the very beginnings of golf in Ireland. The ghosts of Old Tom Morris, James Braid and Harry Vardon fill the landscape.

Faldo described the Old Links at Ballyliffen as 'the most natural golf course I have ever seen', and club members will tell you proudly that the principal architect was Mother Nature! Pat Ruddy and Tom Craddock will concur and confide that it was from such a God-given advantage that they set about the enhancement of Ballyliffen as a new and exciting thirty-six hole resort, with the creation of the Glashedy Links. It measures in excess of 7,000 yards and by all standards it has unfolded as an exhilarating addition to a golfing destination that can no longer be kept a secret!

Donegal — renowned for its scenery and golfing virtues, as shown here on the Glashedy links at Ballyliffin, and at Bundoran, on a clifftop overlooking the Atlantic Ocean.

Luttrellstown Castle in an invigorating West Dublin setting.

Glenlo Abbey, a challenging new course with spectacular views in the grounds of Glenlo Abbey Hotel.

The winners to emerge were Nick Faldo, Bernhard Langer and Sam Torrance, a roll call of modern sporting giants gifted with the credentials to meet the Nicklaus challenge and all of whom were so enthusiastic in their praises that Langer was moved to suggest it as a future Ryder Cup venue. And yet, it is to his eternal credit that the designer, with perceptive purpose, also kept the average player in mind.

Originally the work of James Braid the lovely Tullamore has undergone a major refurbishment programme.

Depending on your standard, you take your choice of teeing ground and find reprieve in the experience of a golfing lifetime. Beautifully shaped fairways, contoured greens and, inevitably, water are seen to play a part. Holes 2, 3 and 4 set the tone amid the leafy ambience. Holes 11, 12, 13 and 14 heighten the senses. Holes 17 and 18 bring it all to a fitting crescendo. You will know you have been in a fight. And you will be all the more fulfilled by it!

The vast wooded Mount Juliet estate, of course, offers more than a lone golfing experience. This is a luxury resort — the award-winning hotel originally built by the Earl of Carrick over 200 years ago. Today, Mount Juliet House retains that aura of eighteenth-century grandeur, but further offers the more informal option of the Hunter's Yard, which is the centre of Mount Juliet's many sporting activities. The Yard embraces the chance to fish in the well-stocked River Nore, enjoy shooting at a clay target academy, indulge in some archery, or horse ride and walk along the ambling trails in one of Ireland's most invigorating woodlands.

When Arnold Palmer had finished his work at the K Club he reflected for a while on the balcony overlooking the spectacular 18th hole and mused: 'We could draw for 100 years and still not come up with as good a vision!'

Ever since, he has been readily complimented for a design that reflects so admirably on Ireland. There is a treasure-trove of great holes, touched in some way by the presence of water. The River Liffey, which flows through the course, is especially to the fore in the playing of the 7th hole, named Inis Mór, a stand-alone 600 yards-plus par 5 of rare design, where the river fronts the green and dares you to ignore its presence.

Later, the many lakes that festoon the invigorating countryside put you to the pin of your collar, most especially in the daunting finish of the climactic last four holes. Finish with the same ball and you are in credit.

As with Mount Juliet, the millions of pounds spent on creating the K Club have facilitated the end product of an all-embracing resort. Fishing in the Liffey or in any of the plentifully stocked lakes is also a feature, while historical Straffan House, of award-winning five-star repute, stands as an inviting centrepiece.

Quite literally, a mountain of superlatives can be used when it comes to describing Ireland's latest golfing gems.

County Wicklow is known as the Garden of Ireland and, appropriately, it provides a home for a course heralded as the Garden of Eden: Druid's Glen. The fantasy golfing architect in each of us would readily cherish the brief given to Pat Ruddy and Tom Craddock — to create one of Ireland's finest parkland places to play! With an unrestricted budget, the challenge was inspirational. The end result is that the intended objective has truly been attained.

The innate spirit of Druid's Glen quickly captured the imagination of Eamonn Darcy. At first glance, Ireland's Ryder Cup hero was moved to exclaim: 'Augusta may have its Amen Corner, but at Druid's Glen they have created a complete litany of golf hole thrills — it's just unbelievable.'

Perhaps he was referring to the richly landscaped valley that houses, end to end, the eye-catching par 3 8th and 12th holes, amid the blooming flora and the cunningly designed water features.

It is within this captivating glen that you will find the sacred site from which Ireland's most expensive club — it costs £25,000 to join — takes its mystical name. It is a Druid's Altar, a preserved stone holy table of pre-Christian worship which stands on a hillside overlooking the 12th green.

Or maybe Darcy included also the defiant dog-leg 13th hole, again highlighted by water. And what of the 17th — a stunning par 3, about 205 yards, the ball being aimed (hopefully) to an island green? Then there is the wonder of the 18th. The challenge is awesome. A tough drive uphill to start with. Only then can you evaluate your chances of getting home in two. More often than not,

the strategy is for a cautious lay-up; but even then there is no reprieve as the pitch is aimed at a green fronted by not one, or two, but three shimmering lakes, one cascading atop the other in a design concept never seen in Irish golf before.

Set in the former Woodstock estate and farm, Druid's Glen is a golfing paradise, with Woodstock House, converted at a cost of £2 million, recapturing the splendour of times long past. The stately mansion, originally built around 1760, to this day features classical columns and exquisite plasterwork on ceilings and cornices.

In the same family of ownership, Druid's Glen has a sister in St Margaret's. Another new and exciting parkland creation, it is within easy reach of Dublin Airport and has also been elevated to the top rank of Irish golf courses in a very short time. How else can it be when the par 5 18th hole, ever threatening a watery grave, gains the accolade from Ryder Cup ace Sam Torrance as being 'the best finishing hole I have ever seen and possibly the strongest and most exciting in the world'.

St Margaret's — another new exciting parkland creation, close to Dublin Airport.

'Augusta without the azalea' was, even if somewhat overstated, an instinctive reaction at first sight of Rathsallagh, in County Wicklow. The magazine *Golf World* was sufficiently moved to proclaim it as a future venue for the Irish Open. Further, its merits were endorsed by the great Australian, Peter Thomson, when he came to perform the official opening of the imposing new clubhouse.

Rathsallagh, endorsed by the great Peter Thomson.

Rathsallagh is set spaciously in countryside renowned for its horses, where Peter McEvoy and Christy O'Connor, Jnr, have exacted the highest dividends from a rolling landscape featuring much mature timber, natural streams and lakes. There is a wonderful variety in the type and direction of the holes, stretching almost to 7,000 yards, coloured by an abundance of flower and shrub.

Much the same applies at Powerscourt. If ever a place offered itself up for conversion to a golf course it is this popular tourist attraction, whose stately home, ornamental gardens and waterfall have long been a place of rare beauty. Used as a location for films such as *Henry V*, *Excalibur* and *Far and Away*,

the advent of an eighteen hole course is a fitting addition. Suitably, designer McEvoy has spotted the full potential on the foothills of the Wicklow Mountains, and Ireland has discovered another place of golfing honour.

Fota Island, also by the partnership of McEvoy and O'Connor, Jnr, comes from the same background of excellence, a new creation encompassing the best of old traditions. The club is located in the heart of a 780 acre estate which is included in the 'Inventory of Outstanding Landscapes of Ireland'.

Furthermore, the spacious estate is home to the Fota Wildlife Park and Arboretum, which itself attracts 200,000 visitors each year. The unveiling of such a new quality golfing venue in this environment truly adorns the reputation of nearby Cork City and instantly presents itself as an exciting option to be used as a major tournament venue.

Considering that less than one per cent of all courses in Britain and Ireland are of genuine links variety, you can well take account of the tumultuous praise being heaped upon the precious land acquired by Pat Ruddy for the creation of the quite magnificent European Club amid the dunes at Brittas, slap on the Wicklow coastline. Similarly, on a line further north to the neighbourhood of the renowned Baltray Club in County Louth, there has been due praise for the unveiling of Seapoint.

Here, Ryder Cup ace Des Smyth and his partner Declan Branigan have exacted full dividends from the rare opportunity offered them, as they set about capitalising on the territory at Termonfeckin and adding a further golfing dimension to the area.

The same architectural team also showed marvellous perception in their work at

Set amid a Wildlife Park and Arboretum — Fota Island presents itself as a prospective venue for major golf events.

Powerscourt Golf Course is a fitting addition to famous Demesne in beautiful County Wicklow.

Waterford Castle. Unique in Irish golf in that the eighteen hole course can be reached only by means of a ferry across the estuary of the River Suir, the island awaits as a sanctuary from the madding crowd.

The golf facility is nestled in a picturesque setting flanked by the ivy-clad granite-walled castle, once occupied by medieval monks but now adapted as a palatial hotel. Marketing people will tell you there are many islands and many castles in Ireland, but nowhere in the world is there anything quite like 'The Isle of the Castle'. It's hard to argue.

In point of fact, the south-east region of Ireland has become quite a golfing haven. Across the river from atop the fairways of the Waterford Castle course, your golfing appetite is further whetted by the sight of Faithlegg. Once more you will be taken by the tranquillity it offers. The course was designed by Paddy Merrigan. He has done a fine job on a lovely site, where water is a feature and

Waterford Castle and its Par 3, 16th — unique in that it can only be reached by means of a ferry across the River Suir.

where the final holes amid the trees and rhododendrons have been strategically cut out to create a suitably fitting finale to your round. Three pars to finish and you have played well!

In the same corner of Ireland, the new Dungarvan Golf Club set against the backdrop of the Comeragh Mountains and containing no less than seven lakes, the Dunmore East Club overlooking the harbour of fishing renown, and the West Waterford Gold Club, are further additions to the longer established Waterford and Tramore courses. In the case of West Waterford, an added dimension of value is that the eighteen holes were designed by Eddie Hackett.

When the venerable Eddie enthused, 'I was given the opportunity to design a great golf course in a unique setting,' he certainly was seen to keep his promise, given the maturing nature of a course nestling within

picturesque sight of the Comeragh Mountains to the east, the Knockmealdowns to the north and the Drum Hills to the south. Added visual effect is provided by the Brickey River, although you may not quite appreciate its presence throughout the back nine holes!

Bearna Golf and Country Club, on the outskirts of Galway City, is an inviting new eighteen hole course built on typical Connemara moorland and commanding magnificent views of Galway Bay, the Clare Hills and the Aran Islands.

The latest gem to adorn Ireland's Atlantic coastline is to be found in far-away Carne on the Mullet Peninsula, near Belmullet in County Mayo. Designed by Eddie Hackett, Europe's final outpost has been created on ancient commonage as a community project.

Set amid incomparable beauty, the par 72 course of pure links turf features a series of elevated tees which are designed to exploit the picture postcard backdrop of Blacksod Bay and a string of Atlantic islands.

Elevated tees and plateau greens are a feature at Carne Golf Course in Belmullet, County Mayo, with backdrops over Blacksod Bay and the Atlantic islands of Inishkea and dramatic Achill.

A feature of the new nine hole links course at Castlegregory in Couty Kerry is the facility it has unwittingly provided towards the propagation of the natterjack toad.

Prior to the laying of the course in 1988 there were no pools on the site, until course architect Arthur Spring devised what may now be one of the most unique holes in the game.

In building a large pool to act as a feature for the 160 yard 9th hole, he discovered to his delight that the water would also act as a breeding site for the natterjack toad, hence 'the Toad Hole'.

Now the lake is probably the biggest breeding site of the toad in Ireland.

Arthur Spring is one of Ireland's new and more successful course architects. Also in his portfolio are new courses at Craddockstown in County Kildare, Woodstock and East Clare in County Clare, and in his native County Kerry, the Kerries in Tralee and Beaufort in Killarney.

The Toad Hole at Castlegregory in County Kerry, now propagating the natterjack toad, pictured before and after the introduction of a special water feature.

The leafy splendour of Slieve Russell nestled in the natural drumlin and valley landscape of County Cavan.

Neighbouring Wexford is where Philip Walton cut his architectural teeth. He can be proud of what he has achieved at St Helen's Bay, with its final hole standing on top of the cliff partly overlooking Pirate Cove, out to Tuskar Lighthouse and also Rosslare Harbour with its busy car-ferry port.

This is a holiday area of repute, augmented by the popular Rosslare Golf Club, a true traditional links almost 100 years old, and further embellished inland by the progressive Wexford Club with its

commanding views of the Saltee Islands and the Blackstairs Mountains.

A more typical by-product of the new image of Irish golf can be found, unexpectedly, in the natural drumlin and valley landscape of County Cavan. Here, business entrepreneur Sean Quinn is finding himself well rewarded for the enterprise of building a 150-plus bedroom hotel, also encompassing a 20 metre swimming pool, leisure facility and conference centre.

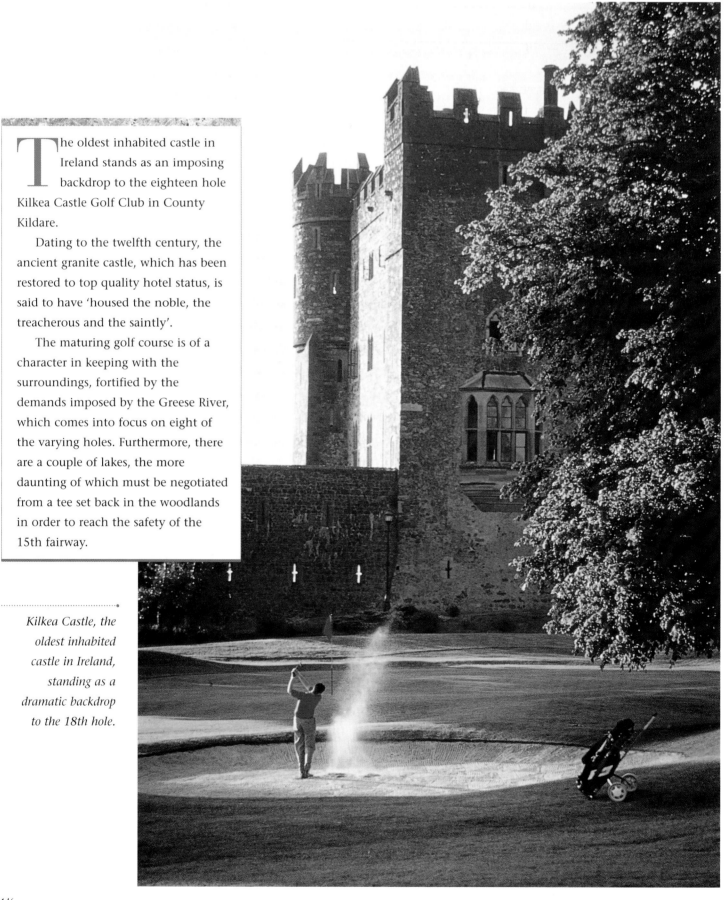

The oldest inhabited castle in Ireland stands as an imposing backdrop to the eighteen hole Kilkea Castle Golf Club in County Kildare.

Dating to the twelfth century, the ancient granite castle, which has been restored to top quality hotel status, is said to have 'housed the noble, the treacherous and the saintly'.

The maturing golf course is of a character in keeping with the surroundings, fortified by the demands imposed by the Greese River, which comes into focus on eight of the varying holes. Furthermore, there are a couple of lakes, the more daunting of which must be negotiated from a tee set back in the woodlands in order to reach the safety of the 15th fairway.

Kilkea Castle, the oldest inhabited castle in Ireland, standing as a dramatic backdrop to the 18th hole.

In terms of golf, the magnificent landscape offered designer Paddy Merrigan rich potential. To his everlasting credit he has done a marvellous job. The delightful, rolling parkland terrain has been sculptured cleverly to produce an array of thrilling holes. Take heed of the names allocated to some holes: the Mourning Pond, Watergate, Risky Rud, Heron Haunt. Self-explanatory!

Two lakes, connected by a stream, are amply utilised in the varied hole sequence that has won the heart of Christy O'Connor, Snr. 'One of my criteria in judging a golf course,' he said, 'is that you get pleasure from it each time you play. I played Slieve Russell four days in a row and can't wait to get back.' That sentiment stands as rich endorsement of one of Ireland's finest new creations, which gets its enchanting name from the local beauty spot called Slieve Rushen.

The combination of building luxury hotels in association with quality golf courses has been a feature of the commercial contribution to Irish golf during the past

The County Tipperary Golf and Country Club in the heart of the Golden Vale, just six miles west of the Rock of Cashel, incorporates the eighteenth century manor — Dundrum House Hotel — former seat of the Earls of Montalt and now converted from being a convent and orphanage.

The leaded windows of the old chapel have been left intact as a feature of the 19th hole in their new and elegant surroundings. European Tour stalwart Philip Walton designed the popular eighteen hole parkland course which he conceived cleverly from amid the heavy woodlands of an ideal setting through which flows the Multeen River.

fifteen years. This trend also takes account of the quite splendid Portmarnock Hotel and Golf Links.

Situated alongside the more esteemed Portmarnock Golf Club which, of course, endures as the Republic of Ireland's premier place to play, the 'new' Portmarnock evoked this response from one leading golf architect after playing a round: 'When God was making the world He laid out the dunes and terrain so that one day a great golf links would be sited here.'

The spanking new Portmarnock Golf Links, sited on the rugged duneland on the east coast just north of Dublin City and where St Marnock established his monastery.

Opulence and golf go hand in hand at the luxury Ashford and Dromoland Castle hotels.

As with Ballybunion Old, there is an eerie sense at first sight, given that the opening hole is framed on the right-hand side by the graveyard and final resting place of St Marnock. By the time you finish you should be fulfilled by the unique challenge, because throughout the tantalising trail that nature so kindly bequeathed, you will be enormously invigorated by your round of golf on as good a links terrain as was ever plotted.

In due deference to the clever eye of the architects, it can be said that the final three holes at the Portmarnock Links are a marvelous finishing crescendo. The 16th sets the tone. It is a left-to-right dog-leg from a high tee in the dunes from which you must carry at least 150 yards in order to clear a deep hollow that lurks with destructive intent. At the 17th, behold a dramatic uphill par three with a large bunker dominating the front left of the green and a severe fall-off to the right. Then gingerly onwards to the 18th, demanding further accuracy off the tee and presenting the deceptive approach to a well-guarded green which nestles in a natural amphitheatre, with the imposing — and inviting — Portmarnock Links Hotel as an eye-catching backdrop.

In Dublin's western suburbs you will also be enchanted by the sight and challenge of the new Luttrellstown Castle. The castle itself dates back to the fourteenth century and in its preserved five-star splendour it is used privately as a hotel by the rich and famous.

The parkland course, thankfully, is not of the 'monster' variety, albeit no give-away. Luttrellstown weaves its way around two ornamental lakes at the 9th, 10th, 11th and 12th and is a welcome new addition to the facilities in the greater Dublin area.

Nobody quite told St Marnock! When he established his monastery on the rugged duneland along the east coast just north of Dublin City, he could hardly have foreseen that one day his name would be dedicated to a mecca of golf. If he had had an eye for the game, he would not be displeased with the brushwork of Bernhard Langer, in association with Stan Eby, because, while it is a totally new creation, the Portmarnock Links course manages an uncanny blend of the traditional perspective with all that is best in modern architectural design.

Killarney is renowned as Ireland's most beautiful and famous tourism resort.

The Killarney Golf and Fishing Club has commissioned the noted architect Donald Steel to build a third course to augment the existing O'Mahony's Point and Killeen courses of world repute.

Golf is now seen to be a central part of tourism in the area, as many other new courses have been built in order to meet the demands for more playing facilities.

Beaufort Golf Club, with its 200-year-old trees, twelfth century castle ruins, fairy lios and rolling hills, is an impressive new option. Dunloe, a pay-as-you-play concept, set spectacularly in the Gap of Dunloe and with views down to Killarney's lakes, is another. So too is Ross Golf Club, an inviting nine hole layout with a clubhouse that commands a 180 degree mountain, woodland, lake and castle vista.

The settings for the upgraded playing facilities at Parknasilla in the grounds of the Great Southern Hotel and similarly enjoyed by the new club at Killorglin also endorse the claim that Kerry holds the distinction of combining the best golfing facilities with added scenic merit!

The much loved Dooks Golf Club which is steeped in golfing tradition . . .

. . . and the new Killorglin course, both help to make County Kerry a golfing mecca.

*The view from the first green on the Killeen course at picturesque Killarney, over the
lake and onwards to the Macgillycuddy's Reeks.*

From the aeons of time and spectacular beyond belief. It is difficult to argue as you behold the sight of the Old Head golf links, close by the ancient harbour town of Kinsale, County Cork. The unique site, perched hundreds of feet above the ocean, is a national monument and an ancient royal site, fortified by a castle at the narrowest part of the promontory, with history traceable back to several centuries before Christ. The Old Head was included in the 'Inventory of Outstanding Landscapes in Ireland' as being a 'narrow coastal headland with spectacular cliffs of geological interest'. The course was designed by a combination of Ireland's greatest golfing heroes and recognised international contemporary design experts — led by Joe Carr, Ron Kirby, Paddy Merrigan and Eddie Hackett.

Golfer alone on the links.

INDEX